7/20

A MORE
PERFECT
REUNION

Also by Calvin Baker

Grace
Dominion
Once Two Heroes
Naming the New World

A MORE PERFECT REUNION

Race, Integration, and the
Future of America

CALVIN BAKER

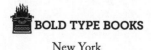

BOLD TYPE BOOKS

New York

Bold Type Books
116 East 16th Street, 8th Floor, New York, NY 10003
www.boldtypebooks.org
@BoldTypeBooks

Printed in the United States of America

First Edition: June 2020

Published by Bold Type Books, an imprint of Perseus Books, LLC, a subsidiary of Hachette Book Group, Inc. Bold Type Books is a co-publishing venture of the Type Media Center and Perseus Books.

The Hachette Speakers Bureau provides a wide range of authors for speaking events. To find out more, go to www.hachettespeakersbureau.com or call (866) 376-6591.

The publisher is not responsible for websites (or their content) that are not owned by the publisher.

Print book interior design by Amy Quinn.

Library of Congress Cataloging-in-Publication Data
Names: Baker, Calvin, 1972– author.
Title: A more perfect reunion: race, integration, and the future of America / Calvin Baker.
Other titles: Race, integration, and the future of America
Description: First edition. | New York, NY : Bold Type Books, 2020. | Includes bibliographical references and index.
Identifiers: LCCN 2019058186 | ISBN 9781568589237 (hardcover) | ISBN 9781568589220 (e-book)
Subjects: LCSH: United States—Race relations—History. | Racism—United States—History. | African Americans—Civil rights—History. | Social Integration—United States.
Classification: LCC E185.615 .B268 2020 | DDC 305.800973—dc23
LC record available at https://lccn.loc.gov/2019058186

ISBNs: 978-1-56858-923-7 (hardcover), 978-1-56858-922-0 (e-book)

LSC-C

10 9 8 7 6 5 4 3 2 1

Now let us, by a flight of imagination, suppose that Rome is not a human habitation but a psychical entity . . . in which nothing that has once come into existence will have passed away and all the earlier phases of development continue to exist alongside the latest one.

—Sigmund Freud, *Civilization and Its Discontents*

CONTENTS

PREFACE

"You're the first *extranjero* who has ever been in my home,"
he said. Maybe he meant foreigner; maybe he meant
stranger. I wasn't sure. It was late in the evening and I didn't
ask him to clarify. We were in the living room of a one-story
cinder-block building, a brick-by-brick undertaking still taking shape. The kind of house you build yourself—as circumstances dictate—according to your courage of imagination to
meet them. It was my final night on the island, near the southern coast of Mexico, between Cancer and the Equator. It was
five hours by rough roads to the nearest city and two hours from
the market town, where people from the smaller villages went to
find provisions: hardware, appliances, an honest agent to broker
what affairs they might have with the larger world. I had arrived
there largely by chance, in search of a quality of solitude vanish-
ingly rare.

There were only a few hundred families on the island,
mostly fisherfolk who had moved in after the logging companies
stripped the area of hardwood and left behind the road they had
constructed to transport the timber to market, which went by
way of the sea. They said that before Cortés arrived, there was

an older habitation there, but only a few traces remained, turning up only when someone was digging deep to lay the foundation of a new building.

His wife had taught me some words in Mayan, and their preteen children wanted to know if I'd seen an outlandish Hollywood movie whose protagonist shared my name. We were all in stitches as they recounted the plot. Besides that, our conversation was about history, land rights, property values, and climate. It was a conversation that might be had anywhere, especially between Alaska and Tierra del Fuego: property, laws, value, policy, culture, change. All of these were flowing, perhaps more in one direction than the other. Nothing about any of it felt remarkable except the prelapsarian beauty of the island and neighbors who greeted even a stranger on roads where one might walk a mile without seeing anyone. But I have spent a lot of time walking around talking to people the powerful never listen to. We were speaking Castilian, a lingua franca with a local inflection, which was neither of our mother tongues. We live, after all, in an age of global humanity.

Far from being a new phenomenon, the current historical epoch began across the Atlantic world in the fifteenth century, when Europe reemerged from the isolation of the Dark Ages, reencountered her neighbors in Afro-Eurasia, and soon ventured to the Americas on the same trade winds.

We are only too familiar with the accidents, massacres, and tragedies that later unfolded, but the ability to travel great distances also sparked the modern global movement of people that has increased exponentially in the ensuing years. However one may feel about it, at some unseen inflection point we crossed the event horizon, and this process became irreversible. We will never again be anything other than a global species.

Before the Portuguese reached the River Senegal, before Marco Polo met Kublai Khan, from the very beginning of anatomically modern humans 300,000 years ago, and even earlier, people were already on the move. First, we traveled from East Africa across the continent, then, 70,000 years ago, journeyed eastward into Asia. Forty thousand years ago, according to current consensus, humans ventured west into Europe and finally, 15,000 years ago, populated the Americas.

Africa, Europe, and Asia occupy a single landmass, of course, a fact we often overlook. At various points in geological time, America was also connected. Those early hunter-gatherers were following the herds in search of resources, as were the farmers who spread from the Tigris-Euphrates Valley. So too were the early Portuguese, who wanted to circumvent Muslim control of the trans-Saharan trade routes in search of gold. It wasn't this simple, naturally. History is sometimes an arrow, sometimes a wave. But it seems that human nature and the shape of the globe mean we were, one way or another, fated to meet again.

More recently, as colonialism was felled and democracy spread after World War II, this migration shifted from the periphery of empires to metropolitan centers, as people sought relief from collapsing economic systems based on exploitation. In our own time, as centers of power and capital continue to shift, this movement has multiplied across the entire world. People now relocate for economic, environmental, political, educational, familial, and purely personal reasons, at a pace and scale that make this movement a central fact of contemporary life. It

is also a fact that threatens and overwhelms "traditional" societies and eighteenth-century ethno-national ideas of states.

I am glossing over a great deal, but the tension between
global humanity and ethno-nationalism, along with its frater-
nal twin, race, seems to me the fundamental backdrop against
which current events are unfolding. This owes in large degree
to the fact that for most people race, a flawed, antiquated explanation for the physical differences among people, codified in the
eighteenth century, remains in this century the central totem of
the self. Certainly, to speak of things I know best, this is true in
my own country, which so often proclaims itself the light of the
world. It does not matter that the alleged science behind race
has long since been proven as erroneous as a flat Earth; it long
ago became a foundational myth of who we are, taught early and
reinforced often. In the United States race is, even more than
national tribe, a useful fiction to explain to us who we are and
how we are oriented toward the world. As such, it is less a valid
idea than an organizing belief. In this case a form of magical
thinking impervious to fact but ever threatened by truth.

Our current notion of race began on the dim edge of the
Middle Ages, before the universe was heliocentric, before we
knew gravity. At best, it was a primitive, tentative grasp toward understanding the physical world; at worst, it was a way
of asserting the primacy of one tribe over another. When it was
considered in earnest by science, it was initially rejected. James
Cowles Prichard, a physician and opponent of slavery from
Bristol who was the leading British scholar of race, wrote in
an 1813 book entitled *Researches into the Physical History of Man*
that "on the whole, it appears that we may with a high degree
of probability draw the inference, that all the different races

into which the human species is divided, originated from one family."[1]

Race's true usefulness, however, was not to science but as a technology of war, of depopulating continents, seizing the wealth of others, erasing the beauty and wisdom of unknown cultures, enslaving people, and otherwise dividing humanity for imperial gain: all the material forces we talk about so often, which we now so clearly know threaten to destroy the world.

Just as crucially, beneath all this there is a racial ego that goes beyond reason and even material greed. This racial ego, which asserts the superiority of one person over another based on nothing except phenotype, has always informed both individual and group self-perception. It continues to perform this function in our own time, even as interconnectivity has increased, science has debunked race, and most of us, if not always our presidents, kings, queens, and ministers, embrace the diversity of peoples and cultures as belonging to a universal humanity equally worthy of respect, even awe.

This isn't a book about globalization, or colonialism, or even race, but about a concept I think is of more vital importance to the world as it is and not as it was: integration. It is a deceptively simple term, one we think we understand based on our received ideas, be they positive or negative. However, as we'll see, the idea of integration has always been too frightening, too threatening to the status quo to ever consider fully, so much so that twenty years into this century we have barely begun to consider what it means.

Although there has been an increasing awareness of the force of the past on the present over the past fifty years, one of the things integration inevitably implies is using this knowledge to dismantle the bricks of slavery and colonialism. It is one of the few tools capable of doing so, where so much prior history has accrued. The present discussion is about the United States, but it seems a short leap of the imagination to see that the implications of this experiment involve the future for everyone.

Yet even in a country so fond of congratulating itself for being the first modern democracy, the few moments when we have come close to relinquishing the colonial past have always produced a quick retreat from what is, properly understood, the most radical, transformative idea in US politics. The reason we recoil, in language, in policy, in the lives we lead, is because the transformation that integration is capable of upsets not only abstract institutional systems of governance, economics, and culture but also our deep, private selves.

The collective institutions of society that perpetuate racism, and its role in identity formation, are also the same apparatus that creates each of us. Because of this, it is impossible to fully know their effects. We are too implicated. Because these systems are so unfathomably deep within us, the thought of doing away with them shakes us to the core. Instead of talking about integration—the solution to the problems we have inherited—we retreat, or are forced back, into the familiar, threadbare language of race, which in turns soothes us, prompts despair, lulls us into half-measures as we tell ourselves that this is all that can be done for now or that the problem is too complex.

The problem is complex. It is also imminently solvable, if we reframe it in a way that lets us look without flinching. Quite simply, our problem is not race—that tired, old arithmetic that keeps us forever circling the point and has carried us, arguably, as far as it is capable—it is the calculus of integration, dismantling the *problems and structures* that race actively creates.

For hundreds of years, integration has been the clear-eyed, logical goal of the civil rights struggle. For an equal length of time, it has been something Americans have sought to avoid. Fifty years after the last meaningful effort toward civil rights, the country remains overwhelmingly segregated and over-whelmingly unjust. Integration, which is nothing less than full equality, is a state that can exist only where the line of race is not eternally re-created.

Because the race line gives such comfort, integration is an idea that, shockingly, has been abolished from political dis-course. Instead, we discuss piecemeal problems and piecemeal solutions. Because of the racial ego, on the individual and group level integration remains something few can conceive. In a so-ciety in which the material and psychological race line was not eternally re-created, it would be as plain as day. Instead, it is a radical proposal.

The aim of these pages is not to be proscriptive. The way to abolish the race line is simply to abolish the race line. The policy measures necessary to do so may differ according to the area of society, but in a country that has deployed a New Deal and a Marshall Plan, they are neither mysterious nor particularly deep. What's deep are the lies we tell and excuses we make to avoid tackling this problem, which, left to its own devices, will destroy the country, perhaps even *wants* to destroy it. The sim-ple reason is that this problem is and has always been the tyran-nical enemy of democracy, and there are a great many more than we care to admit who are perfectly comfortable with tyranny. That should be apparent to all at this late juncture, as recent events have come to remind us.

There is another foe of action, besides the right-wing extremism that has recently been renormalized. It is the compromise institutional liberalism has long made with tyranny in the name of its own comfort, self-regard, and a desire for power and expediency that rationalize any shortcoming. This self-regard seeks to turn the conversation from integration whenever it is raised, to refocus narratives of culture and politics so that they appease narratives of race instead of democracy. It is a politics of negative capability, asserting what those in control of liberal institutions believe and what they deem realistic in order to maintain their own power, not what is necessary to complete US democracy. This sort of liberalism is enmeshed with white supremacy and does its bidding, whatever it may claim its intentions to be.

This book is concerned with the true goals of civil rights and equal citizenship, going back to the revolutionary generation, which have been abandoned after a campaign of massive conservative resistance intended to muddy the waters and thwart the way. It is about what might have been and what might yet be: *if* the generations now alive are bold enough to relinquish the lies of the past, the lies many in power claim as immovable reality, and battle again for democracy.

Of course, the political class and the media class and all those whose livelihoods depend on things remaining as they currently are will argue that none of this is possible. That America is still not yet ready. What they mean in fact is *they* are not yet ready, even though this has always been a generations-long struggle. The transactional systems of governance and commerce suit such people perfectly well, and those who fancy themselves to be part of an American elite are happy to perpetuate the current state of affairs.

If we wish to have a democracy of free and equal people, we must be willing to wage war with all tyrants, whether they announce their intention outright or call themselves friends. Why shouldn't we? They are already at war with democracy and human dignity.

Before introducing what will be for many people, some with the best intentions in the world, an unpopular idea, it may be useful to remember how a system of myths—made-up stories meant to explain something people didn't have any better answer for long ago: some benign, some malign, many flamboyantly stupid—have shaped so much of history. How it defies belief to observe the ways the assumptions of race continue to shape events in a world where we tell ourselves we know better. We do, and we don't.

It is one thing to know something. The real question—what to do with this knowledge—has proved paralyzing for just as long. And so we do as little as possible, to our continued detriment. Already in the early years of the country, thinkers from Jefferson to de Tocqueville understood the emergent system of racial tyranny as the greatest threat to American democracy.

Yet Americans have always, every generation, found a way to live with this tyranny or else to do some of the work and tell themselves that this is all that might be done, that the country is not ready and the rest is a question for the future. We are now in that future. As long predicted, race has torn the country apart again and again.

The work required to change this once and for all is still too threatening to fully engage, even for the liberal-minded. Americans tolerate this tyranny out of a sense of apathy in the face of accumulated "facts on the ground," sure, but also because those old myths serve the majority across the political spectrum. Rewriting them affects not simply the legal system or education system but also the ways our cities and towns are organized, how we do business, the stories that fill our screens. Ultimately, however, it represents an ego threat to who we understand ourselves to be.

There have been four crucial moments in our history that brought integration to the fore, asking how comfortable Americans were living with one another as opposed to occupying an apartheid state. Each moment offered the opportunity to remedy this, an escape from the original sin and eternal problem of race, if only we were willing to embrace it.

The first such moment was during the Continental Congress, when the tides of revolution recognized slavery as patently at odds with democracy. By all logic the birth of the Republic *ought* to have been the death of both slavery and the racial caste system. There were, we well know, powerful economic forces, built on a triangular trade in goods and capital, with the suffering of others at its base and idolatry of extravagant wealth at its apex, which wished for no such thing as a country of free people. The sheer audacity of a war with England pushed the two sides into union for mutual safety. The North was well on its way to abolishing slavery, but antiblack and anti-native bias had accrued for centuries. It made the most tortured of peace treaties, the first Constitution, with the slave states.

The alliance blew apart, as was presaged, during the Civil War, still the bloodiest in US history. After the war the rights of black Americans would be enshrined in the most significant revision to the Constitution in the country's history. Yet after this de jure victory the country would reunite in ways that de facto denied blacks the rights of citizenship and saw their hard-won freedom violently suppressed in order to appease the former enemy. The enemy has always been within. If blacks were the necessary sacrifice for a quick reunion, the majority of anti-slavery Americans were willing to abandon them as a separate caste. Amnesia soon followed, setting the stage for an ongoing theater of racial awakening—I'm woke; I'm woke—played out by every generation since, but never followed through all the way.

The overthrow of this violently repressive caste system was the long-held goal of the civil rights movement of the 1950s and 1960s. Of course, no sooner had the Civil Rights Act of 1964 been signed into law than both committed racists on the right and their passive enablers on the left found ways to thwart the new legal protections afforded to African Americans in the key areas of labor, housing, voting, and education.

The tools they used were old ones, sharpened over centuries of oppressive practices: political propaganda, legal attacks, manipulation of the voting system, prisons, white flight to segregated enclaves, underfunding schools, private discrimination, and a media and cultural sphere built to affirm and reinforce narratives of segregation and race. They were so effective that the language of compromise—"multiculturalism," "diversity"—has replaced the more straightforward and honest promise of integration.

Affirmative action, a term popularized by President Kennedy in Executive Order 10925, meant simply using the power of government to ensure that employers did not discriminate against black candidates for jobs, as was then common, open practice.

Unlike integration, this addressed only one area of harm. Tellingly, discrimination in the workplace remains a problem that demands attention sixty years later.

For most Americans the word *integration* conjures images of school busing, the tool initially deployed to meet federal desegregation requirements after the 1954 *Brown v. Board of Education* decision. In response, Virginia senator Harry Byrd led a campaign called, none too subtly, "Massive Resistance," which united federal, state, and local power in thwarting desegregation. It continued into the 1970s.[2] Today, people reflexively think that school busing failed or that it is something black people rejected. It did fail, in the same way a bicycle might be said to fail after someone has stuck a stick in its moving spokes.

In business a shifting marketplace has led many to embrace terms like *diversity* and *multiculturalism*. These ideas often include African Americans, but they just as often can be manipulated to produce a United Nations we-are-the-world display without tackling the real underlying problems of US society.

Reparations, another reemergent buzzword, which has gained new currency of late, deserves credit for reigniting a conversation about exactly what the present owes to the past. Reparations have a much simpler, less threatening goal than integration; their aim is not to bring African Americans into the full bounty and opportunity of US society. But I would suggest integration as a truer field in which to hold any discussion about the future of race in America because it acknowledges not only the pain that America has caused black people but also the fundamental right of black people to participate fully in America on equal terms without special pleading or explanation. In a country so expert at creating exemptions whereby the social contract does not extend to black Americans, any proposal that says it does is where the real resistance will begin.

We are at present in America's fourth moment of full-throated national reckoning with race. Quite simply, the election of a black president, the most visible *symbol* of racial progress in decades, led to the backlash of white bigotry, a core of meanness that has been ever present but has now gained enough new strength to ascend the national stage without masking what it is. It wasn't the only determinant, of course, but it was the most powerful factor in the white vote. As we grapple with the problems, large and small, of race in the wake of this, we have come to realize these problems are once again a naked threat to democracy itself. There is nothing alarmist about saying, "If we do not turn our attention to integration, this particular experiment in democracy is unlikely to survive."

Integration, in simplest terms, means full rights of self-determination and participation for *all* African Americans, as well as for *all other* excluded groups—most obviously, indigenous peoples, Latino Americans, Asian Americans, and Arab American communities—in *every* facet of national life. What I mean when I say self-determination is not only the right to life, liberty, and charting your own future but also the right to be respected as you are. A government and society that are on your side as a citizen, not against you.

Integration is the only remedy to the racist state and is the deepest threat to the entrenched racial order, because in order to abolish the problems and injustices of race, one must abolish the function of race. At its simplest this function serves to divide America between populations that receive the rights and respect due a citizen and those that do not. We have been talking in circles about the problem long enough. Integration goes to the root.

This is the line at which US democracy has always faltered, even though the Enlightenment architects of democracy thought they had discovered a force that was stronger than tyranny and was destined to bend history and embrace all of humanity. Race has always been the crook in the arrow of this history: no amount of theorizing, or reliance on time alone, will ever right it. Democracy will never succeed, and indeed is necessarily doomed to fail, until this false exception has been abolished.

I do not believe there is a magical formula that will solve all the problems of the twenty-first century, which have already overwhelmed the twentieth-century infrastructure and the ideas that preceded it. But I know that all answers to the question of America run through integration, which must be understood as the central challenge of our time and the foreseeable future. Although this book is about the United States, the problems are global ones. If we can't fully address them in the birthplace of democracy, the future everywhere will remain entombed by the myths of the past.

Introduction

THE LIE OF DEMOGRAPHICS

This is the next and the more profound stage of the battle for civil rights. We seek not just freedom but opportunity. We seek . . . not just equality as a right and a theory but equality as a fact and equality as a result.

For the task is to give 20 million Negroes the same chance as every other American to learn and grow, to work and share in society, to develop their abilities—physical, mental and spiritual, and to pursue their individual happiness.

—Lyndon B. Johnson, 1965 Howard University
Commencement Address

On a recent fall afternoon one of my brilliant friends, who had been my professor twenty years earlier, e-mailed to see if I was available for dinner. I took it to be a social call as I went to meet him later that week at a West Village restaurant once frequented by the writer Richard Wright and his wife, Ellen, when they lived nearby. It was among the few neighborhood establishments that would serve an interracial couple in 1950s

New York, even in one of its most liberal enclaves. We both liked the restaurant for this. The food and the wine list are also good, but nice meals are common in New York. We went to feed the ghosts, and invisible histories.

We spent most of the evening catching up on mutual acquaintances and talking shop, the ebb and flow of creative life. As we neared the end of dinner, he turned abruptly silent, which was not entirely strange. It was the kind of friendship comfortable with silences. "Listen," he said when the conversation resumed, "Yale is going to offer you a job. You should take it."

It was only then I understood it had been a job interview. Despite the honor, he knew that even if I had spent much of my life around universities, I had a critique of the most common approach to the things I study. "Can I actually teach?" I blurted out skeptically before I could stop my tongue, in a way that, in retrospect, fills me with chagrin.

"If they're hiring you, it means they trust you to do whatever you want," he said as we left the restaurant. "As far as the rest of your concerns, you don't have to worry about any of that, not with the kids you'll be teaching."

The Yale English faculty is housed in a pair of conjoined Romanesque and neo-Gothic buildings through whose labyrinth of offices, classrooms, and courtyards one could trace much of the intellectual history of America. I don't think it controversial to say that over the years, more original minds have gathered in those rooms than nearly anywhere else in America. It also happens to be one of the few institutions that have survived the colonial era.

The students awaiting me that January afternoon turned out to be some of the most gifted one might hope to meet anywhere. If this were a book from an earlier generation, this is where I would stop to reflect on my discomfort or offer some piety about how lucky I felt to be there. The truth is I've spent most of my life feeling odd, halfway in and halfway out of everything. But as the semester wore on, I've seldom ever felt as much at home.

My fortune was to have inherited two of the most competitive courses on campus, which meant that I had my pick of students across English and the related departments of American Studies and Comparative Literature. I chose students on merit, and as a group they happened to look exactly as one would want a meeting of the brightest people in twenty-first-century America to look.

Ines, whose name, like the rest, I've changed to protect her privacy, was a Chicana from the borderlands in Arizona, the first in her family to go to college. Peter, a quiet blond boy from Rhode Island, was a second-generation Yalie and, deservedly, a leader in the student community. Dawn was an African American woman from Georgia, who also happened to be Latina. Adaolisa was from the West Coast, the daughter of a Ghanaian father and white Canadian mother. Rachel was active in the campus LGBTQIA community and was committed to social justice as she tried to understand her own identity and place in the world. David, a Jewish kid from the heartland, was conspicuously nice. He never missed an opportunity to demonstrate what a good guy he was, or how sensitive to others. Frances, who sat at the other end of the table, was also Jewish but had an atheist's relationship to religion and the complex ethnic feeling of the third generation: perfectly assimilated in most contexts yet hardened in the face of any perceived anti-Semitism. She grew impatient whenever David fastened his identity to Judaism and angry whenever she heard a slight. Lucy was a New England WASP, a standout at boarding school whose familial expectations about what being at Yale meant ran counter to her own mind and imagination, which were far more interesting and nuanced than her background suggested. All of them were.

They were also, like many people born after the civil rights movement, part of a still-developing experiment in integrated education, which in this moment meant feeling empowered enough to speak up for themselves, whatever their identity, while demanding equal respect. I loved them for that. Even if some of the logic of their arguments was not yet sound, their feelings and the substance of their critiques were incredibly right-minded.

But even in a room with so much talent and goodwill on the multitudinous sea of identity, looking, as we are so often reminded, the way our American future is supposed to, they were, every last one of them, still so trapped by their *own* identities that they could not see one another fully. How could they? They had only just met. A syllepsis—which means something both literally and figuratively true.

Like a great many people, their individual concerns, and the language in which they had been taught to express them, often blinded them to one another, even as they gave voice to the frustration of being unseen. They could speak about, and advocate, their personal positions in the most sophisticated, confident terms. However, they didn't have enough experience with those who were unlike themselves to be able to see through one another's eyes. Good intentions and fellow feeling are not the same thing. Political speech is not the same as full human articulation. It is the difference between a party platform, which describes the outline of a vision for national life, and a novel, which tells of the deep interior of an individual consciousness amid the hidden mechanisms that really govern society. There is a great deal that our current political language fails to capture, and therefore to affect.[1]

I'm not sure how possible it is to truly understand anyone else's deepest life, but I do know that the ways identity, including racialized thinking, affect and shape us run deep. At some point, for all the good it's done in giving us a political language for injustice and to help define a national dialogue about injustice, the politics of identity and race also traps us in a feedback loop of *representing* the self without deeper understanding. My grievance versus your grievance. My "own truth" versus another's. It's easy to nod and say the right thing without listening or speaking of the deeper self. Sometimes we lack awareness. Sometimes the pain is too much. Sometimes the rage. Sometimes the shame. Even when we inhabit spaces that look integrated on the surface, we bring prior experiences of race and segregation to the ways we see and interact.

The first class met on a snowy afternoon during the day that Donald Trump, a president less qualified than Jefferson Davis and yet a product of American democracy, was inaugurated. The students, who had grown up in Obama's America, despaired of what should be done now that the excitement of those years had come crashing to a halt. They felt the world had told them an infinitely cruel lie about what this country is and feared what might become of them in a society that had returned so quickly and gleefully to patriarchy, misogyny, racism, xenophobia, inequality in all its forms. "We are going to do our work," I said simply, knowing the full answer to their question was more complex than I could answer in the first class. Maybe even more than could be told in a single semester. But I trusted that the deep work of real reading and writing did hold the answers. My job was only to provide more subtle tools in the most lucid space I knew how to activate.

What gave me any sense that I was qualified to explain any of it, beyond a lifetime of reading, was that I had spent most of my life grappling with a host of the same problems: of feeling the world was opening up to include those who looked like me or shared my concerns, only to learn that much of the country wished for no such thing and even those who thought they did still did not understand properly what that meant. I will admit I used to think we were further along; it is only recently I understood how new and strange genuine encounters across lines of identity, those engineered divides of history and humanity, truly are in US society.

Because of my own experience, I was aware of the power of treating my students the same and holding them to the same standard whatever their social identity. I also knew they were not the same and understood the burning hotness of having someone traduce your individuality because they could not disentangle you from whatever their idea was about your group and, just as bad, receiving some well-meaning blandishment from someone in authority, or else a high-minded theory, which in the end is only that, a theory. It is exactly at this theory of equality that we as a society have chosen to stop.

Midway through the semester, the living complexities began to reveal themselves, namely the human differences beyond the surface of meritocracy and the truth about the world we live in, and the current sociohistorical moment. First, David wrote something that all the women in class objected to, accusing him of objectification. Some vocally, others with silent disdain. He defended himself by saying the right things, fearful of social shame. He was more mortified of what would happen if he told the whole truth: that he did not mean to give offense but also did not fully understand what he had done wrong or how to make amends.

A week later, Dawn wrote something about her life as an African American woman, dismissing the other students for failing to understand it. She was partially right. Literary studies are organized in antiquated ways. Some of them can't be changed. Some of them have already been changed, but English departments still haven't caught up to them. This means the serious students of color have been for generations learning and integrating two canons, one in which they are included and one in which they are not.

Later still, Frances was told that something she said was a product of her Jewishness, when this was not the case at all. She was being reduced from a person to a member of a group. Peter did something brilliantly subtle about violence directed at gay people, without politicizing it, causing the others to miss the point entirely. It was, like the other misunderstandings, a failure not of politics but of reading. Among a great many other things, reading well requires that we see what is before us instead of simply relying on what we believe we know.

Adaolisa, who was as sensitive as she was gifted, felt she was being exoticized. Lucy thought everything was queer and anyone who denied it was homophobic. Ines, who was used to having schoolwork come easy to her, began using her background as an excuse for sloppy work, in a way no one had ever bothered to call her out on for fear of being seen as insensitive, condescending, or worse. Her problem had less to do with her background than with the defense mechanisms gifted kids resort to when things become more challenging than they are used to and intelligence alone is not enough. After conferring with a colleague, I ended up assigning her enough extra work that most graduate students would have protested and most departments would claim was too high a standard. To her enduring credit, she did all of it.

All of them were conscientious people, and, with few exceptions, I made a practice of addressing whatever offense had been given, received, or perceived in office hours after class, where none of them could be judged or feel vulnerable before the others. Both because I believed what each of them needed to hear was individual and because I wanted them to remain open and vulnerable before one another. Without that, none of us could ever learn anything, especially not the things we would rather pretend we already know than admit our frailty. At least I know my first instinct is always to cover up defensively in environments where I feel unsafe or afraid.

Like my students, I had grown up in a society integrated in some ways, segregated in others, and had been educated in spaces that prided themselves on their multiculturalism (in reality a murkier operation involving teachers who often had little experience of integration beyond the handful of students who passed before them). It was a time that felt on the verge of change. What surprised me was how similar the language my undergraduates used was to the language we used. Little, if anything, new had been said in the twenty years between us. Older people had told me the same thing once. As much as I resented them for it at the time, it eventually entered my hard head how much all of this was a generation-over-generation conversation, one that stretches back to the very first generation to call itself American.

The sentiments and the problems are the same. Only the names and faces of the people have changed. But also the numbers. My parents grew up in a time of black firsts. I grew up in a time when black people in spaces privileged as white were usually few and far between. The only black kids, or a small enough cluster to fit at a single table in the lunchroom. Now there are more, but still not as many as there should be. The problems in the ghetto, of course, remain the same, too. And that there are ghettos.

The first waves of the civil rights movement began to right the abject harms of racial oppression, only to see them become ever more resistant and ever more subtle, reaching into law and economics, but also deep into cultural and physical space, and inevitably into personal realms that no law should ever reach but that nonetheless demand interrogation.

In the case of my class, wherever they came from and whatever their other concerns, none of them wanted any part in reproducing the structures of oppression: structures they recognized more completely than a great many older people but still struggled to know how to escape. Compounding this, they also wanted to succeed. Many were savvy enough about "the way things work" to understand that even exposing the full extent of their worries, of their ignorance in front of one another, laid them open to charges of being naive, prejudiced, or worse. They simply said the right things publicly. As a performance it was good enough for most situations, but each of them intuitively knew the difference. We can all sense when someone sees us and when someone does not.

This is the same unresolved state in which liberal society at large currently exists. We know intellectually that the world is unjust and do not wish to be instruments of oppression. Yet if we are honest, most of our lives implicate us in ways we do not know how to free ourselves from, or else know but lack the steadfastness. This complexity is what we politely ignore or treat with platitudes when we talk about race, diversity, multiculturalism, and intersectionality. We have lost focus on the tangible systemic problems and, in this distracted state, the necessary sense of purpose to resolve them.

Instead, in liberal as well as conservative spaces, we pride ourselves on how far we have come from slavery, from lynching, from the overwhelming physical, material, and psychological oppression we politely call segregation. We declare our good intentions instead of measuring ourselves against the goals we wish to reach, as one does when one is serious about something.

Speaking truth to power, as the old canard goes, means nothing unless we live those truths fully. America has always been a deeply dualistic construct, one free, honest, and democratic and the other brutal, larcenous, and repressive. Saying we oppose these things, or addressing the problem reactively at the site of whatever new tragedy has unfolded, will never be enough. We must understand the completeness of the problem and the full effort required to solve it.

The extrinsic benefits of an elite education include access to opportunities, and they serve, especially for students from historically excluded groups, as social proof of worthiness. As a corrective for the ways prior environments have taught us to see, or not see, even if there were enough seats in such places to address the issue at scale, it remains perfectly possible to inhabit these spaces without meaningful interaction with those who do not share one's background. It is equally possible to congratulate ourselves for the appearance of multiculturalism without challenging the prejudices we have internalized and know better than to speak aloud. Because so many of the notions we receive from our society are so deep and so entwined with our identities, it is often a fool's errand to try.

I wish I could offer a fail-safe formula to eradicate unconscious biases in a foreshortened time period. The question of whether it is possible for us to see one another and ourselves across social divides is one of the complex questions in contemporary culture, informing nearly everything else, either implicitly or explicitly. I happen to think that it is largely possible, even perfectly possible. One sees it so plainly in artists such as James Baldwin, Toni Morrison, or Philip Roth when he cared to and, each by another remarkable path, critical minds as different as Harold Bloom, Jacques Derrida, and Edward Said. Without getting too esoteric, I believe that this vision turns on the ability to dissolve the world and access one of the better, more transcendent selves. This conflicts with our usual materialism and will to power, and is more in tune with the view that we are limited beings.

However, for those already programmed by the system, the mask of falseness, whereby we pretend to see, to understand, to know better than we do, runs so profoundly deep—in its vanity, its presumption, its performances now of superiority, now of empathy—and elicits such hostility when it is revealed to be a mask that for most of us regular folk, the answer is similar to whether it is possible to become truly fluent in another language. The younger you start and the more you practice, the greater the chance of success.

As a practical matter, this involves being more aware of the ways that narratives and meanings are produced by their societies, the variety of these narratives, and what they tell us about the desires of society and individual consciousness, including our own. This quest is less abstract than it sounds.

When it comes to race, the cultural borders are especially unstable, which is why they must be continuously reinforced and narratives of authority constantly elevated. This process of policing and reinforcing happens at the individual, social, and institutional levels, and it happens largely in the background of conscious awareness. It is larger and more powerful than the lone individual. Not only can such a system be unmade; its deepest fear individually, socially, and institutionally is that it *will be* unmade.

Whether and, crucially, how deeply this information is received lie beyond the boundary of the classroom. I like to think that my students all became more aware of the complexities of reading and writing, and how manifestly entwined these are with their own social beings in ways that expand who they are and what they are capable of. But a great deal depends on how honest and open they can be with themselves and one another in a cultural milieu that contains so many competing values. If they fail at this, sometimes saying one thing while thinking and feeling another, for fear of social censure or betraying the chink in their armor, well so do we all.

We manage our knowledge and self-presentation according to the demands of the environment. There are some things one can tell students only in a classroom, the earlier the better. There remains other knowledge that cannot be contained in institutional spaces but belongs to the unique intimacy of books.

Before we go on, it is necessary to point out something irreducibly simple, which may strike a few as basic but will cause most people some degree of discomfort. There has never been a race problem in America. The reason there has never been a race problem in this country is there is no such thing as race in this world.

Every attempt to assert the validity of race, whether by the most duplicitous white supremacist or vehement black nationalist, is a deep lie. Every argument built on race, every argument about race, everything ever said about race other than to debunk it is at base meaningless, grounded entirely or reactively in a scientific and social history of white supremacy.

There are many reasons race should be in the center of our national conversation; after all, the effects and desires of racism are too real. It is a myth that inspires actions, systems, people. Still, everything that follows from falseness is necessarily false. Race is the first theorem in the argument that different peoples have different abilities, are worthy of different esteem, and deserve different fates. It is a commonplace defense for evil.

Our society does not have a race problem; it has a racism problem. It has been organized around this falseness since the seventeenth century, an unfathomable amount of time in human terms, but not so much on the scale of history that it cannot be righted.

We know it was the capture of a Portuguese galleon carrying imprisoned Africans to Mexico that brought the first Negroes to the English settlement at Jamestown. Even the name of the vessel comes down to us through the years: the *White Lion*.

We know the Spanish had practiced slavery since the Reconquista ended Muslim rule of the Iberian peninsula and that they began to enslave their former masters. As the Portuguese and Spaniards starting exploring the Atlantic, they carried slavery with them from port to port, like rats, like disease.

We know that at the beginning of the plague years in North America, African and English servants shared quarters and conditions. We know hereditary bondage went hand in glove with the invention of capitalism. We understand that the moral, financial, and psychological need to justify slavery led the early colonists to look to the ancients, to theology, to science, to anything they could to create an ideology of racism. We know its oppression continued long after the Civil War and continues still, so deep is it within the fabric of the society, a fabric from which each individual is cut. We know, from generations of witnesses stretching back to Olaudah Equiano, who wrote the first account of the Middle Passage by one of its survivors, that race wishes not only to steal the body but also to claim the spirit.

As history would have it, we have organized US society and our sense of self around a fiction as baseless as the Easter Bunny, Santa Claus, and the Tooth Fairy. America had a slavery problem, and with it a white racism problem, both of which collided with the concept of democracy. After slavery ended, we faced the problem of how to integrate the newly freed or, as the case may be, how to avoid it. Race, both product and producer of white-supremacist thought, is the crutch that props the whole thing up.

Recognizing race for what it is and what it fully means to move beyond it would be as devastating as it would be for a child to realize all the myths and charades his parents invested so much energy and imagination in upholding are simply not so. One no longer knows what to believe. Letting go of the myth of race would engender a crisis so profound in contemporary Americans that to call it spiritual or existential would be an understatement. But what else is it when we are asked to abandon the gods of our parents and their parents as far back as anyone remembers? If the world understands me as a black man, if I deeply like being African American and have defined myself and my life by it since I had agency to define anything, what am I, besides a maverick or fool, if I let that go?

There are metaphysical answers to that (too convoluted to engage—call it complex consciousness) and religious answers (a child of God), but in our secular, materialist world most of us would say: a human being. However, we all know that what we say and what we do come apart before lunchtime most days of the week.

When it comes to what we call race, our words and deeds are eternally apart. If we relinquished race, I would remain a black American, of course, part of a cultural, historical, and communal experience—but black as I define it. In a society beyond race, blackness would belong, like any other ethnic identity, to my private self and shared cultural experience instead of being a civic state of urgent concern, a social caste apart.

America does not view all people as human beings. In an integrated society we would eventually all be simply Americans, without other qualifiers. We would interact as equals and sort ourselves according to affinities. In a democracy that part of me does not belong to the public at large. Only in a society invested in patrolling blackness down to the ontological level would it even be a question. A nation of free people will do as they will.

But I get ahead of myself. Even as an intellectual exercise, US society is so constricted by racialized thinking that it compartmentalizes its black citizens and the internal functions race serves. The thought of a society not defined by race must first go through the dismantling of racial structures. This is where the contemporary imagination, like the historical one, wants naturally to stop.

Just as the physical world has been segregated to minimize contact with one another, even when we do talk about race and racism we barricade the conversation as a special category apart from other spheres of existence. This allows us to talk periodically about the adverse effects of race as something separate, belonging only to whatever catastrophe has recently unfolded, as opposed to a force, hidden as gravity, affecting the entire field of American life.

This mental and metaphysical segregation allows us first and foremost to avoid thinking about what race has produced in most areas of our lives, then to look for a few affirming exceptions, telling ourselves that this is really the rule. Even when we discuss the effects of racism directly, even when we say aloud that it touches every aspect of this society, we don't actually apply that knowledge to the way we think about the society and act within it. We can point out that schools produce unequal outcomes, then go on about our day without doing anything to address it, fighting for a coveted spot within a system that we claim to know is broken. We recoil when we consider that it might require us to relinquish our own perceived privilege. We may say with our forebrain that we are all the same, but primal conditioning produces involuntary reactions to the contrary. If breaking down the internal, individual forces that give rise to these larger social patterns is so difficult, what hope is there of doing so in the face of much larger forces?

We have been perfecting this avoidance for centuries. By the time the English in America declared independence, slavery was more than 150 years old. It was during the revolutionary generation that Americans first awoke to the magnitude of the issue. Four hundred years later, we are still doing everything in our power to keep kicking that can down time's road, even when we tell ourselves we are having a national conversation about it. America has become expert at co-opting critiques of race and racism, and soothing its own conscience, without doing the real work of addressing the problems it has created.

Integration requires more than mere discussion. The idea of actively integrating the millions of excluded Americans is a goal that traces back to the end of the colonial era and the more forward-thinking members of the revolutionary generation.

It is a concept of the national order that was already deeply threatening, and so nearly impossible to imagine in the eighteenth century. It did not find its true voice until the next century, in the writer and orator Frederick Douglass and his sometime friend Abraham Lincoln. It was Lincoln's assassination that allowed the revanchist forces of an unapologetic South and its northern sympathizers to rewrite the history and goals of the Civil War. By the end of the war, Lincoln was not only opposed to slavery; he had also come to understand that abolishing slavery was only the beginning of the road to equality. Taken to its logical conclusion, this remains the most unsettling, radical idea in modern life, which is why we always stop short of its logical conclusions. A full third of the country, call them neo-Confederates, is fighting vehemently to roll back its partial conclusion. As I write this, the liberal contenders for the American presidency are still struggling to find a language that expresses support for the equality of all in practical terms palatable enough for the country at large to accept, without affirming full commitment to integration. They favor school desegregation but not busing, the only tool that has proven effective. They are against racial discrimination in law enforcement, but they dare not say anything that might upset the current paramilitary police state. The "not in my backyard" cowardice runs through every vein of US life when we dare to speak of dismantling the racist state we inherited. The result is an abstract support for integration while keeping the actuality of integration ever at bay.

What makes integration in America such a unique challenge, but also a distinct possibility, is the uniqueness of American history. Few countries have built a liberal democracy, devoted to enlightened thought, inside of which was constructed a colonial state devoted to the same exploitation, suffering, and abuse as feudal Europe's overseas dominions, nearly all of which were apartheid states of minority rule or built in the aftermath of genocide.

America, as well, was all too recently an overtly colonial state of oppressor and oppressed.[2] In common with other societies constructed along categories of whiteness and other, we find ourselves, as the Black Power generation asserted, in a postcolonial society. The Electoral College, which awarded disproportionate power to the slave states, is an artifact of this. In 2016 Hillary Clinton won nearly three million more votes than Donald Trump. Without overstating the procedural problem, it is literally true that we currently live under minority rule, unable to move beyond the most repressive forces in national life.

As counterintuitive as it sounds to call the United States a postcolonial nation, and as difficult as it may be to accept when talking about what is often called the most powerful empire in history, it is the proper frame to contextualize and understand the scale of what we face. The full truth of the matter is that no country in the modern era has yet overcome the effects of either colonizing or being colonized. This is our challenge.

When European colonization ended in the twentieth century, the French, the English, the Belgians, and the Germans could simply return home and draw high the bridge. When the Civil Rights Act at last defeated America's internal colonialism, oppressed and oppressor were left sharing, always and ever, the same land. If it is a land in which white supremacy is once again ascendant, threatening the core of democracy, it is because it never truly went away. It was silent so long as it got its way, and the Left has been backing down in the face of antidemocratic white appeals to race for over a century.

Not facing it now means to continue living on different sides of the track, in different towns, separate and unequal in public spaces, as well as in the collective imagination, even as we remain interdependent. The problem that the revolutionary generation always understood would be this country's most difficult has been inescapably hard upon us, and so, fifty-five years after the Civil Rights Act, it remains. Even in America's most liberal institutions and public spaces, what passes for integration is still only a surface representation, seldom a fully normal, mutually accountable interaction among equals.

For the moment we have settled for the tacit understanding that by allowing a few into majority-white spaces and places of power (in what we call meritocracy), we are collectively freed from the complex problems of the many, which is to say tens of millions of people in this country. There has always been a class of exceptional African American people in colonial societies, whose existence serves to buffer the interests and self-regard of the status quo from the suffering of the masses.

Adding to our confusion is the fact that we Americans have always weighed ourselves and our politics against the extreme. This creates the hidden gravity that, as it always has, pulls the allegedly more liberal side intimately near. The inner narrative is "We're not like X" or "Y is way worse." These are reactive not proactive positions, by which I simply mean we define ourselves by what we are not, not by who we are and what we wish to accomplish. Or, as Douglass reminded Lincoln every time he saw him, it is one thing to abolish slavery and another entirely to integrate the majority of black people into society. That is the challenge of this moment and the most meaningful test of the American future. We can face this fact or continue to tell ourselves increasingly baroque lies as the country ossifies once and for all into a partial democracy.

As the country grows more diverse, we have resorted to telling ourselves that shifting demographics will solve our problems, a fear that has led conservatives to want to build a wall around the country, enact new poll taxes, and gerrymander political districts to dilute the power of voters. But even without these nefarious, antidemocratic efforts, demographics alone will not solve the problem. It runs too deep, beyond our ability to see. The only balm that will make this wounded society whole is a new understanding of and broader commitment to integration. Symbolism, exceptionalism, hoping for a future victory that requires no sacrifice in the present are not enough.

Part I

THE SHADOW BEFORE MEMORY

They have black skins and curly hair (not that that amounts for much as other nations have the same).

—Herodotus, *The Histories*

1

WHEN WE WERE ENGLISH

The mind is its own place, and in itself
Can make a Heav'n of Hell, a Hell of Heav'n.

—John Milton, *Paradise Lost*

An all-reaping fire scythed the tobacco fields in the pre-dawn morning as Anthony and Mary Johnson battled to save their summer harvest on the eastern shore of Virginia, in a country not yet as old as they were.

The Johnsons were natives of Angola, on the southwest coast of Africa, who had arrived on the first slave ship to the country that would one day, years in the future, be America. Jamestown, the first settlement and their landing point, was founded in 1607. Twelve years later the Johnsons were landed aboard the *White Lion*, after the Spanish vessel stealing them to Mexico was itself captured by a tribe called Englishmen.

After working off their term of servitude, an estimated fourteen years, like the approximately 50 to 75 percent of early

European immigrants who arrived to the colonies as indentured servants, the Johnsons went on to amass 250 prolific acres as free folk. Their two adult sons owned and cultivated six hundred more on the adjoining lands. The damage to the farm that morning was catastrophic, laying waste to all they had toiled for in America.

In light of such hardship, something remarkable happened. Their neighbors in Northampton County decreed the Johnsons exempt from taxes for the rest of their lives. An act of God. A human kindness. A simple demonstration of small-town decency and frontier solidarity that would be unthinkable in years to come.[1]

As the colony of Virginia morphed slowly into a society built on the backs of African slaves, the treatment of blacks would grow increasingly inhumane, until they were no longer even people anymore in the eyes of the law and their neighbors who wrote it, but property to be bound and held forever.

Colonial records are notoriously scattered, but blacks made up 13 to 40 percent of the colonial population of the southern settlements, and black freemen are estimated to have constituted as much as 13 percent of the black population, living largely like the Johnsons as independent farmers among their English neighbors without legal distinction.[2] The expectation at the time was that they would assume the customs of their new country, acting and being treated as "black Englishmen."

Forty years later it would be illegal for them to even live in the colony, after the Virginia Assembly passed a bill in 1691 requiring newly freed persons of color to be removed from the jurisdiction. Their mere presence was too disruptive for the system of race-based slavery being built. After all, a flourishing free population gave lie to everything that would come to be said about those with darker skin.

A decade after this first discriminatory law banning them from settling in the colony, blacks were stripped of the right to hold public office; black, indigenous, and mixed-race slaves were declared to be property; interracial marriage became a legal offense; any child born to a white woman of a black father was subjected to an indenture of thirty-one years; and all blacks were forbidden to vote—underlining the fact that in the early country, before the racial structures that would define and damn us, there existed no glint of an era when blacks could possess all the rights of English citizenship and social interaction among individual members of the various groups was governed, as one might expect, by natural law.

"Yet I cannot see," a lawyer named Richard West wrote in the seventeenth century, as the legal distinctions casting Africans out of society were being written, "why one Freeman should be used worse than another merely upon account of his complexion."[3] For the English, being English, the distinction was in rank. In the New World the answer was simpler: Virginians who aspired to the wealth of the European landed needed labor to work the vast new land, and so committed themselves to slavery and racial tyranny to support it.

In a depopulated colony, where the economy was dependent on labor-intensive cash crops, love of wealth outshone any other concerns. Other self-justifications would come later. In the beginning it was the simple, pressing need for workers. As de Tocqueville would note a hundred years after the fire on the Johnson farm, when slavery was rooted deep, "Generally speaking, men must make great and unceasing efforts before permanent evils are created . . . but it afterwards nurtured it-self, grew without effort, and spread naturally with the society to which it belonged. This calamity is slavery."[4]

Slavery across the main of Europe had been abolished hundreds of years earlier with the spread of Christianity. In the ancient world the nascent church grew in no small measure by taking the side of the slaves, who were approximately 35 percent of the population and far more numerous than slave owners. In the New World the church mostly sided with the oppressor, a moral reversal apparent to this day.

Although the Spanish were the first to introduce the prac-tice to the Americas, it soon spread across the hemisphere as European powers vied for the wealth of the world. The Portu-guese ship *São João Bautista*, which was attacked by the *White Lion*, with the people we know as the Johnsons aboard, was one of untold skirmishes between English and Spanish vessels as the two countries fought for primacy in the Atlantic. Harassing one another's ships was common practice, whether the cargo was sugar or gold. Africans simply happened to be aboard this one on that day.

After plundering the *Saint John*, the *White Lion*, along with another ship called the *Treasurer*, raised sail for Virginia, where she docked at Port Comfort and her human wares were sold to a group of local Dutch merchants in exchange for provisions to see them safely home to Liverpool. The Dutch baptized the Af-ricans, then transported them to Jamestown, where they were sold to a group of Englishmen, who had never before bought or sold a human life. A group of Angolans, aboard a Portuguese ship headed to a Spanish colony, was captured by Englishmen, sold to the Dutch, and finally transferred to the Americans. It was already a global trade.

It is simple enough to explain the economic reasons that slavery, once started, became common practice, eventually removing 12.5 million people from Africa, killing 1.8 million in the Middle Passage, and landing 10.7 million across the Americas. Of those 10.7 million, 388,000 humans were sold in English North America, which though never the geographic epicenter of slavery was as mean a place as any other.[5]

After the importation of slaves was abolished in the United States, in 1808, there would be a second, internal slave trade that boomed when cotton exploded in the nineteenth century, tearing apart families and people who had been settled nearly a hundred years. By the time of the Civil War there were nearly four million forced laborers in the United States, and, as if to compensate for the fact that it was never the white-hot center of the trade, slavery in the United States was not one apocalypse but two, each with its own violent reaping.

In light of all this, one sees the comfort it would give someone who lived in a slave-based society to declare Africans a lesser kind of human, to blame them for the problems that would ensue from this crime for hundreds of years, to declare America great, the heritor to Rome, while cultivating blindness to what it had wrought ever after. All became logical defense mechanisms in the way that even the illogical makes sense once you understand what someone is trying to hide.

In America the terrifying, beguiling shadow has always been the darkness between the America that exists and the America that might be.

One clue to this inheritance might be found by asking what would compel an Englishman—which is what those in colonial Virginia still were—to submit to the mortal sin of slavery in the first place. Slavery, after all, had been illegal in England, as it was in the rest of Western Europe, for a thousand years. And even at its height, in the English holdings of Jamaica, Barbados, and the southern colonies of North America, it would never be embraced in the mother country, where it was said that to breathe English air was to be made free. Perhaps it was simply easier to accept that which is kept out of sight. Race and its evils have always been kept psychologically offshore.

England at the time was a place of tenant farmers, with varying degrees of rights, from those who were almost gentry to those bonded to the land for life, living in thatched huts; bustling cities teeming with sewage and disease; and, of course, the full magnificence of Renaissance thought and culture. The reign of Elizabeth brought a period of peace and stability, marked by overseas exploration and burgeoning awareness of the larger world. It was also the time of Shakespeare, who gave English literature its first glimpses of the cosmopolitan world to come. In plays such as *Othello*, staged as Virginia, then a backwater colony, welcomed the *White Lion*, Shakespeare questioned the role race was beginning to play in the world, and he found the world wanting.

In common with all of Shakespeare's works, there are many ways to read *Othello* and many ways to misread it. How one interprets this play reveals a great deal. At base, *Othello* is about a stranger mistreated, undone by his own psyche and those who claim to be friends. Othello is both a man of singular accomplishments, respected by the society around him, and a foreign *other* alone in an untested world that no isolated individual can ever master.

Near the tragedy's beginning, Brabantio, a Venetian aristocrat and father to a daughter named Desdemona, is outraged upon learning his daughter has married Othello, not because he is a Moor but because she betrayed her father in not seeking his permission before her marriage. Iago, an army officer who reports to Othello, has informed Brabantio of the elopement for reasons of his own. He is accompanied by his coconspirator Roderigo, whose own romantic interest in Desdemona has been spurned. Together they claim that Othello used witchcraft to seduce Desdemona. Although Othello had often been a guest in his home, Brabantio's mind soon begins to run the racist course Iago intends. This is the true witchcraft only race can perform, to lift an Iago above an Othello.

Called to defend himself before the Duke of Venice against the charge of stealing the nobleman's daughter, Othello does so by recounting their courtship, testifying that his new wife fell in love with him after hearing his life story. From the details he provides we understand how impressive and resilient is Othello, who has been given charge of leading the Venetian navy: "She loved me for the dangers I passed, / And I loved her that she did pity them."[6]

Given a choice between Othello—heroic, vulnerable, large and in charge, or as his enemies would have it, an "extravagant stranger"—and Roderigo—highborn but dissolute and vindictive—most honorable women would do the same. "I think this tale would win my daughter, too," the Duke counsels Brabantio as he adjudicates the case.

When Desdemona's account of the courtship matches that of her new husband, disproving the charge of seduction, Brabantio withdraws the case and welcomes him: "Come hither Moor. I here give thee with all my heart."[7]

Iago, however, is just getting started. The crux of his grudge is that Othello passed him over for a promotion, which he clearly does not deserve. Iago is not only vainglorious, insubordinate, and unfit for the rank his pride aspires to; he is a master study in villainy, one of the great lowlifes in all of literature. His character, and the nature of all men like him, can best be summed up in his own declaration: "I am not what I am." All things false a man may be rest coiled within that line. He manipulates his wife and his friends. He is disloyal and deceives his commander, his lords, his prince, by extension country, not to mention any personal principles of valor or truth, so much that he belittles those who are honest.[8] He is not only rotten; he is proud of his talent for deceit. "I am not what I am." Racism is his first tool.

In league with the equally jealous Roderigo, Iago sets out, like Lucifer, to avenge his wounded pride. The cut for both men is unbearable. Othello has not only bested them; he is better than they. The audience's sympathies are immediately with the Moor, in a way that would soon be impossible in the America that was taking shape.

It's worth pointing out the setting of the play is Italy, not England. Venice, situated on the Mediterranean, was in close communion with the Ottoman Empire and North Africa and, by trade, far Asia and sub-Saharan Africa. It was already cosmopolitan, like Rome before it, in a way that London was only beginning to catch up to. *Othello*, based on a true story, serves as a harbinger of the world soon to come.

Roderigo and Iago are scoundrels by nature. Racism is a feature of their scurrility but tangential to its foundational function in their character. They hate the guy for being what they cannot be; because he's black and a foreigner, they attempt to use that against him. ("I hate the bastard, and he's black, as opposed to I hate him *because* he's black.") But their seventeenth-century slurs—"extravagant freewheeling stranger," "lascivious Moor," "tupping the white ewe"—still resonate with the language of modern racism.[9] In contrast, the honorable characters practice what in the modern world would be called meritocracy. All of this reveals a society in which racialized attitudes were already forming, and just how old these attitudes and libel against the black body are, but it was still not yet a world ruled by race. Whatever else might be said about him, Othello is a free man in a position of honor and is in fact honorable.[10]

Because Venetian society has chosen to judge Othello on his merits and not his skin, Iago's racial scaremongering falls on largely deaf ears, and he must resort to other forms of trickery. Iago and Roderigo are unworthy on a fair and equal battlefield for what their vanity tells them is their due, damning them to the audience. Their ego is greater than their ability or merit; worse still, they view treachery as a virtue. This is the treachery that would become the law in England's North American dominions.

Across the Atlantic, whole nations of Iagos were declaring themselves worthy, warping the rules to their own advantage and spreading the poison of race for centuries to come. In the

New World even Iago's self-knowledge would become a truth to hide from: "I am not what I am."

In the United States, black actors were long forbidden from playing Othello because the role entailed an interracial kiss. In the United States, the play would be misread as a cautionary tale against interracial marriage. In the United States, blacks could not be portrayed as courageous or worthy. In America, there could be no Othello. American governance would enshrine Iago's point of view. In the American theater of race, Iago, in all his treachery, is the actual hero.

In modern American life the person most often compared to Othello is the football player O. J. Simpson, a black man accused of killing his white wife. That is what stands out most for a society steeped in racialized thinking. But it misses a major point. Venice was the commanding naval power of the Mediterranean world. Othello was admiral of its fleet. This wasn't sport. This was war. A better parallel might be to imagine Colin Powell sabotaged by Michael Flynn. Or Donald Trump prevailing over Barack Obama. Race turns the world upside down, has no rules but its own unruly emotions, and calls false things true.

In the United States, it would be three hundred years before a black actor, Paul Robeson, could play Othello in a major production. It would be a generation after that before an American interracial love story would come to the screen, in 1967's *Guess Who's Coming to Dinner*. Both productions were hailed as groundbreaking in their day, but they were only a return to the normal course of human society when it isn't actively impeded by racism. We imagine we are making progress, but really we have only just caught up to where the racialized world began.

As slavery gained purchase, along with a legal and social framework to support it, the Johnsons quit Virginia, where they were no longer welcome, and moved to Maryland, where they struggled to build again from the beginning. On the institutional level, *Othello* could not have been written in America between the seventeenth and twentieth centuries because the military was segregated for most of that time. It would not be until the twentieth century that blacks would hold highest command. On the legal level, the marriage between Othello and Desdemona would have been prohibited in most states under widespread miscegenation laws until 1967. For most of the country's history, the couple would never have been allowed their day in court.

On the social level, Brabantio would not have needed his thoughts twisted to harbor ill will toward the Moor. It would have been the case all along, and Brabantio would scarcely have entertained Othello as an honored guest in his home. There would have been no need for Iago to resort to trickery to achieve his ends. The couple would never have met, and if they had, Othello would have been lynched. In America there could be no Othello. As one of Ernest Hemingway's characters would have it three hundred years later in one of the consequential books of the American canon, "Othello was a nigger."[11]

This is the perverse course the English in America took when, shorn of civilization, cast into an unknown wilderness, increasingly unwelcomed by the indigenous inhabitants, and intent on getting ahead in what was a most precarious endeavor, someone shook hands with the captain of the *White Lion*.

There's no meaning beyond this, unless one believes that, in an absence of social contracts, religion, education, or other improving force, it is human nature to do whatever one can get away with. This is the problem that race solved. It allowed one to maintain a sense of self as an Englishman and not a barbarian, as the actions would imply.

There's no evidence of any other design on the part of the early Virginians but opportunism. Once set in motion it became the governing law of the new society, functioning apart from the larger concept of democracy in a land that imagined itself both sanctioned by God and heir to the democracies of antiquity. Long after English hegemony ended, and no ethnic group could claim a monopoly on power, it continues to do so under the banner of whiteness.

Outside of race there was, according to the early ideals of democracy, a directional arc to history. If you subscribe to this view, then you also believe that when race entered the American mind, it functioned, as it continues to function, counter to history itself.

The institutions created to wall it off from rational thought, and the burgeoning Enlightenment, arrived in law, in culture, and in custom to the extent that now in the twenty-first century whenever we break away from such customs to claim a universal democracy, it becomes, like the rulings that struck down the so-called miscegenation laws and segregation in public places, cause for liberal celebration.

It should not be. There is nothing progressive about people in the twentieth century marrying whom they wish. Every liberal victory of this type is a partial repentance of colonial structures, an event we are supposed to take joy in, as opposed to the full restitution of natural rights, masking the fact that after four hundred years of oppression America has yet to extend the full social contract to blacks. This theft of their rights was the flaw in the design of America we have been struggling to right or struggling to resist ever since. What steps we may take toward fixing it are long overdue, not something one gets special credit for or cause for moral vanity, at least not if you begin with the assumption that people truly do have the same abilities, same dignity, and same rights. Viewed from this perspective, we are a hundred years and more behind schedule and have no claims to victory, only work to do.

But the habit of clear-eyed democratic behavior has yet to take root, either in policy or on the psychological, institutional, and social planes that have been warped in service of racial segregation. Like our thinking about race and the social instincts we inherit, each of these planes is warped still. So much so that most times we don't even recognize the tilt, which serves to seduce us into taking measure by that which is false, not that which is true.

2

THE TOLL OF INDEPENDENCE

When I reflect that God is just, I shudder for the future
of my country.

—Thomas Jefferson, private diary

Among the passages excised from Thomas Jefferson's original draft of the Declaration of Independence is an ex-
coriating denouncement of slavery, which he claimed England
had forced on America. In the deleted paragraph he accuses the
mother country (or "stepmother country," as they were by then
shading it), in the person of King George, of "cruel war against
human nature itself, violating its most sacred rights of life and
liberty in the persons of a distant people who never offended
him, captivating and carrying them into slavery in another
hemisphere or to incur miserable death in their transportation
thither."

He was livid when it was cut, blaming its removal on an
alliance between the Carolinas, Georgia, and northern shipping

interests, which all profited greatly from "transportation thither." The names of the conspirators in this alliance are available to us if we search, but they are not the people we talk about when we talk about the architects of America. The people we refer to as Founders all *believed* in universal rights. The only thing keeping them from achieving this was other Americans. Sometimes one and the same person.

Over the course of his lifetime, Jefferson, one of the largest planters in Virginia, held more than six hundred people captive at Monticello. He referred to them euphemistically as "labourers," and over his lifetime emancipated nine, six of whom we know were his children.[1] He was what nowadays might be called a real piece of work.

Despite his intellectual opposition to slavery and his support for a gradual process of abolition, which he came within a vote of achieving as governor of Virginia, Jefferson came by his wealth through inheritance from his father and father-in-law, and was dependent on slave labor. He had tastes he could not afford and lived above his means, styling himself, like his milieu in general, in the manner of European gentry, who took their own cues from the nobility. He was ever plagued by debt.

As Virginia's governor after the Revolution he led a push to ban the importation of slaves, which Virginia passed in 1807, a year before England did the same, and ahead of the federal Constitution. As president he tried to prevent the expansion of slavery to all new American territories.

In his private life he lived in a relationship with one of the people he owned, Sally Hemings, for four decades after his wife, Martha, passed away. He and Hemings had six children together, all of whom Jefferson would eventually liberate.

Jefferson never married again, and Hemings's windowless living quarters adjoined his own. As with many relationships it's impossible to fathom the terms of the decades-long deal between them, which began when Hemings was about sixteen. Whatever their particular cocktail of intimacy and interdependency, it was, God knows, a strange brew, even by the standards of the "peculiar institution." It was also far from uncommon. When the original slave codes declared a child's status, unlike in England, to be determined by the status of its mother—the offspring of a free Englishman and a bondswoman (who by fiat cannot give consent) was also bonded—they were addressing a practical concern, not a theoretical one.

Jefferson's legitimate children and grandchildren knew of his and Hemings's arrangement, as did his friends and neighbors. So apparently did most of the country, as it became a source of news articles and controversy during his presidential campaign. After he died, as his myth grew and the Confederacy claimed him as their own, his descendants through the Martha line would deny the relationship for generations, until DNA testing proved otherwise. Some of them denied it even after the facts were proven, craving, like many people in the later years of the country, their own make-believe truth and history.

It is a perfectly American story, embodying the southern duplicity in which a genteel facade masks a barbaric reality, as well as northern "civility" in which right-sounding speech goes hand in glove with feelings of racial superiority and oppression. Four decades is longer than most marriages, but whatever contentment Jefferson may have felt at home was in direct conflict with his role in society. Hemings, of course, had no place in society.[2] The simplest human joy—a happy family—was tainted.

If it was an unhappy family, it was unhappy in a uniquely American way.

"Nothing is more certainly written in the book of fate," Jefferson commented in his autobiography in 1821, "than that these people are to be free; nor is it less certain that the two races, equally free, cannot live in the same government. Nature, habit, opinion, have drawn indelible lines of distinction between them."[3] The sense of psychological and intellectual torture and compartmentalization in those brief words is thick enough to cut. In the first draft of American democracy even the man holding the pen was trapped in an untenable compromise.

This American conflictedness suffuses even the words "are to be free." One might read the statement "are to be" as the future tense or as a commandment he lacked the will to follow. His own internal contradictions and paradoxes mirrored the society around him, but also the way we have looked to the revolutionary legacy in the years since, turning it round and round like half a glass of water, instead of filling it the rest of the way.

The obvious duality between democratic ideals and an odious business model that contained the antecedents to modern finance and corporate special interests united the North and the South economically. What all of it would mean to the future country deeply troubled many in the revolutionary generation, significant southerners as well as northerners.

According to Benjamin Franklin, "A disposition to abolish slavery prevails in North America, that many of Pennsylvanians have set their slaves at liberty, and that even the Virginia Assembly have petitioned the King for permission to make a law for preventing the importation of more into that colony. This request, however, will probably not be granted as their former laws of that kind have always been repealed."[4] Sixty-five years later, in the generation after independence, John Quincy Adams observed,

> The inconsistency of the institution of domestic slavery with the principles of the Declaration of Independence was seen and lamented by all the southern patriots of the Revolution; by no one with deeper and more unalterable conviction than by the author of the Declaration himself [Jefferson]. No charge of insincerity or hypocrisy can be fairly laid to their charge. Never from their lips was heard one syllable of attempt to justify the institution of slavery. . . . and they saw that before the principles of the Declaration of Independence, slavery, in common with every other mode of oppression, was destined sooner or later to be banished from the earth.[5]

Adams, the sixth president and the first from the generation after founding, is an invaluable witness to the American purpose, testifying from three vantages at once. His father was John Adams, the second president, who had a long, complex friendship with Jefferson and who, in fact, assigned Jefferson the task of drafting the Declaration of Independence. The younger Adams would have had not just privileged information about the written record but also apostolic access to the private conversations and utterances of the founding generation. His argument helps us understand not only what the Founders said in private, as well as in public, but also what the first generation to inherit

America understood those teachings to be. Adams himself was an abolitionist.

I used to be among the camp he chastises, regarding those who professed freedom while participating in slavery as hypocrites of the first order. My thinking has evolved and deepened over time. I think the spirit of revolution in the colonies was close to rapture. The people we think of, North and South, when we say Founders—Washington, Adams, Franklin, Madison, Hamilton, Jay, Mason, Rush, Paine, Jefferson, Lee—were in fact all dead set against slavery and treated liberty with religious seriousness. It was seventy years since the slave codes were codified and, as with taxes, the Founders were absolutely convinced that slavery was part of England's imperial machinery of which they were victims trying to free themselves.

Five Founders went on to serve as president. The first, Washington, manumitted his slaves. John Adams, who headed the committee in charge of writing the Declaration of Independence and served two terms as Washington's vice president before ascending to the higher post, never owned any. Washington and Adams both had virtues and clarity of character that are frankly rarer than we wish to believe.

The other three, Jefferson, Madison, and Monroe, were all Virginians and far more human in their makeup. As governor of Virginia, Jefferson introduced legislation for a gradual but universal emancipation, which Madison supported. It failed by one vote to pass in the House of Burgesses. Another measure, which they both opposed, making it illegal to manumit slaves, did pass. Madison, like Adams, had the kind of mind that stands out even in a room full of genius. He negotiated the constitutional clauses that dealt directly with slavery and was among those who wanted to keep the word out of the document, being keenly aware that to inscribe the term would betray the meaning of the whole endeavor. He was also well aware of the tactical problems of gaining support in the South. He was a slave owner yet seems to have held at least a few of his slaves in human regard, including a man named Billy whom he freed and who later became an important business partner. I have heard the notorious three-fifths clause argued two different ways. The first says he effectively declared that blacks are only three-fifths of a person and that the southern states should gain as much in extra representation. The second says he was reducing by 40 percent the power the South sought. His internal motivations do not seem fully knowable. What he wrote was that it would be "wrong to admit in the Constitution the idea that there should be property in men," arguing that they deserved to be treated as men and not property.[6]

Monroe presided over the bitterly debated Missouri Compromise, which admitted Missouri into the Union as a slave state and Maine as a free state, which preserved the even balance between slave and free states. He also subscribed to the then-centrist repatriation movement and, like Madison, was instrumental in the founding of Liberia, whose capital, Monrovia, bears his name.

Certainly, none of these five men argued for slavery, and all came into it by birth, facing the problem of how to extract themselves from a vice that was entwined with them, with their societies, and with their families. When Jefferson berated King George for foisting it all upon them, he might as well have been talking about his own father.

All of them, like all of us, sincerely believed one thing but faced a fundamental, perfectly relatable question: How do I free myself? Or, for those of religious feeling: How do I free myself from sin?

I believe they thought the best of the human spirit and the principles of revolution were so powerful that once they were free of England, slavery was bound to fall in due order because the American, indeed universal, feeling for freedom was so strong. They saw themselves as making a temporary compromise, in the name of practicality, which they hoped to later revise. George Mason, who wrote the Bill of Rights, is on record as wanting to bar the South from the Union. The majority were convinced of the necessity of a united front in the face of England's superior force. They were anything but cynical, though there were certainly cynics and opportunists in their ranks, and many had the usual amount of self-deceit. I think they underestimated the extent to which racism had shaped them as well as the forces of greed and power arrayed on the other side, and, after taking a bite of the apple, soon learned they had swallowed the devil. They were overly optimistic, and they underestimated the darkness.

Of course, by then the darkness was internal, and rooted deep. Especially for men like Jefferson, for whom the anguish of race was not merely political but personal as well.

Their challenge, like our own, was to escape the legacy systems that produced them and the forces within the new country that continued to actively support those systems. Slavery and white supremacy, as the good people in Northampton County in the early seventeenth century demonstrate, were anything but a predetermined course for America, even after the *White Lion* brought her cargo ashore. Revolution was a fact on the ground that several of the colonies, though not the country, had co-alesced around.

The first generation was trapped within economic insti-tutions and legal codes, but also within social acceptance and customs. As the trickle of people from the eastern Atlantic be-came a flood that overtook the New World, American society nurtured notions of race even in places the law did not. And of course those who actively supported slavery lobbied tirelessly for its expansion across the continent. The advantage to be accrued by owning slaves, and also by thinking oneself better than the poor men and women held captive, became a deep part of the national psyche. Claiming distinction among the races, even af-ter slavery itself was gone, walled you off from the suffering of others and the plausible fear that a country that enslaved Afri-cans could as easily enslave you.

As the existential shadow of blood guilt and fear bled into pseudoscience, it turned to a pathological hatred. Race-based prejudice became the prevailing norm, in the North as in the South, whether slavery itself was present or not. Race served as the totem that organized society. Instead of class, inherited or ob-tained, the New World would be shaped and disfigured, like col-onies throughout the world, by a logic of blood and money. Even at the time, many—and if we take Franklin at his word, most—people knew better. Slavery was widely questioned not only by the learned Founders, who belonged to what would now be called the educated (including self-educated) elite and were steeped in Enlightenment thought, but also by the people at large.

During the Great Awakening, in the years leading up to the Continental Congress, a new religious fervor burned across the colonies and with it the assertion that all were equal before God, that a slave state is never how the world was intended to be. Religion in America would eventually decide that—well, yes, blacks have the same souls—we would all be equal in the next world, not this one. Unlike prior iterations of Christianity, the dominant religious institutions in America would be firmly on the side of slaveholders. But the first voice of God in the new country spoke differently and exerted a deep effect on revolutionary thought.

At the time of the Continental Congress, blacks were more than 19 percent of the population, and as religious feeling was wed with natural law theory, slavery was vehemently viewed in some quarters as anathema to national independence.[7] Indeed, some viewed abolition and independence as one and the same. "During this third quarter of the eighteenth century," writes Winthrop Jordan in *White over Black*, his influential study of race in America from English settlement to the end of the revolutionary era, "many Americans awoke to the fact that a hitherto unquestioned social institution had spread its roots not only throughout the economic structure of much of the country but into their own minds. . . . The antislavery sentiment also represented a process of self-evaluation."[8] This awakening to the problem of race would be performed again and again.

By the age of revolution, slavery had been practiced in America for 150 years, and as Americans debated independence from England, race and slavery became two of the most contentious issues among the colonies. "We have seen the mere distinction of colour made in the most enlightened period of time," Madison wrote, "a ground of the most oppressive dominance ever exercised by man over man."[9] As his language makes strikingly clear, the lie of race was perfectly transparent in the eighteenth century.

The principal holdouts to abolishing slavery by constitutional decree were the same who had resisted it at independence, representatives from Georgia and South Carolina (settled by those who left Barbados, part of the hard-core West Indian epicenter of slavery). In the ratified Constitution the issue was delayed for twenty years, a period during which many hoped they might corral support from all the colonies. But the new states were further apart than they admitted.

The southern delegates, in fact, wished to include in the Constitution itself language that referred to blacks and their descendants as property. Many northern delegates stated plainly they would not sign their names to any document that contained the word *slavery*. Georgia and South Carolina, fearful of abolition, would not agree to any document that did not recognize it.

The Constitution goes out of its way to avoid the word *slavery*, employing three euphemisms in its place: "those bound to Service for a Term of Years" in the infamous three-fifths clause of Article I dealing with representation in Congress, "the Migration or Importation of such Persons as any of the States now existing shall think proper to admit" in the section of Article I that laid the groundwork for abolishing the international slave trade, and "no Person held to Service or Labor in one State" in Article IV, which dealt with the subject of fugitive slaves and would lead in a direct line to the Civil War.

The omission of the word *slavery* from the founding document, as John Quincy Adams made clear years later, was carefully considered: "a fig-leaf under which parts of the body politic might be concealed."[10] The term *fig leaf*, of course, tells of cosmic shame. But also defiance.

Faced with the exigent issue of revolution, the Founders would leave slavery for future times to sort. One of the central questions raised by colonial southerners and northerners alike remains one of the most telling. Can so many free blacks ever be integrated into a society that has come to regard them as inferior? But that would be a question for the future. The immediate matter was abolition, and race was standing in its way.

Among the northern colonies, slavery was already illegal in Massachusetts and Vermont, and the other colonies would soon follow. The largest slavers continued to profit after the ban, many of them eventually turning to investing and banking, running money instead of ships, but still in a trade built on the backs of Africans and later African Americans. This was what we would now call the global economy itself, but momentum was on the side of freedom.

Equality, though, was another matter. As de Tocqueville noted in 1835, "I see in a certain portion of the territory of the United States at the present day, the legal barrier which separated the two races is tending to fall away, but not that which exists in the manners of the country; slavery recedes, but the prejudice to which it has given birth remains stationary."[11] These prejudices would remain overt for a hundred more years. The problem was as evident in the beginning as it is now, but there was simply not the will to address it.

One reason the delegates opposed to slavery were able to make common ground with the southern colonies was because many supported gradual abolition, a process that would allow necessary measures, like job training and education, to be taken to integrate the enslaved population over a period of time. They thought time was on their side.

But, as de Tocqueville suggests, by entering "the manners of the country," racial attitudes no longer had to be taught. They operated independently of law and the institution of slavery itself, had in fact become second nature: social instincts transmitted generation to generation in public as well as private. Despite knowing perfectly well what the problems are, America yet remains so incredibly organized by such beliefs that it seems to be all we can do to diagnose the problem time and again, congratulating ourselves for learning what has always been known.

No matter how false or misleading the lies of race were and even how well we understood this, they had taken hold at the level of national myth, producing our psyche, our actions, and the world being created. Race, the false notion used to justify slavery, also inculcated in the white imagination a feeling of inherent superiority, which became central to white American identity. It was a subliminal phenomenon that allowed and continues to engender very real material outcomes.

Alexis de Tocqueville captures the essence of this when he notes, "There is a natural prejudice which prompts men to despise whomsoever has been their inferior long after he is become their equal."[12] Whether or not it was natural, the same sentiments would continue to inform social, institutional, and psychological interactions for two and a half centuries.

At founding, many who saw all of this clearly were too far in advance of a society that was not yet ready to tackle the challenge. Among the clearest instructions they left is that the problem would not end where their own chalkboard ran out.

The Constitution nods in this direction of incremental abolition with a clause that calls for the nation to consider abolishing the international trade a few decades further on. When the question was revisited thirty years later, in 1808, the international slave trade was in fact abolished, fueling hopes that full emancipation might be achieved in such incremental fashion. It was merely a matter of time.

Time is a capricious master. Instead of weakening the forces in support of slavery, it reinforced them, as the economy of slavery found new momentum in the cotton boom made possible by Eli Whitney's new technology. Resistance across the South grew in tandem with the profits. As the South retrenched, the cry for abolition also grew bolder. The Civil War, the greatest reckoning the country has ever faced, was, in this view, foreordained.

By the time civil war erupted, which many called the Second Revolutionary War, and emancipation did occur, another ninety years of degradation and slander against the intelligence, morality, and ability of blacks had accrued. Stereotypes against blacks—projections of white behaviors and psychological fears or, like southern manners and liberal bromides, bulwarks to assert individual separateness from the cruelties of a slave-based society—had hardened, along with the real challenges the newly freed faced in access to education, employment, and housing. Race by then dominated not only the social world but also the deep interior of the white self, in ways that were ever harder to see and continue to inform the entrenched structural racism we suffer to this day.

The crux of the matter, then as now, even for those opposed to slavery, was whether and if so how blacks might be integrated into society. A range of schemes were spun about the young country, from gradual, full integration to expatriation in some country of their own in Liberia, out west, in the Caribbean, in South America. Such propositions were seriously considered as late as Lincoln—until Douglass convinced him otherwise—and revived again in twentieth-century black nationalism, beginning with Marcus Garvey, based on the belief America would never be a fair place for black people.

In a society already defined by white supremacy, those who believed in unconditional integration seldom spoke out publicly. However, one prominent voice from the early revolutionary period who did so saw education as the most viable path to solving the problems that race created. "The children of the slaves must, at the public expense," wrote John Sullivan, a leading attorney of the day, "be educated in the same manner as the children of their masters; being at the same schools etc., with the rising generation that prejudice, which has been so long and inveterate against them . . . will be lessened within thirty to forty years."[13]

His argument was so far ahead of its time it would wait another 150 years until it found a receptive audience in the Warren Court's unanimous *Brown v. Board of Education* decision in 1954. By then, yet *another* century and a half of racist law and custom had hardened the problem. There was little new in the remedies that twentieth-century America would propose, only more to undo.

As de Tocqueville concluded,

> These two races are attached to each other without intermingling, and they are alike unable entirely to separate or combine. The most formidable of all the ills that threaten the future of the Union arises from the presence of a black

population upon its territory; and in contemplating the cause
of the present embarrassments, or the future dangers of the
United States, the observer is invariably led to this as a primary fact. . . .

As soon as it is admitted that the whites and the emancipated blacks are placed on the same territory in the situation
of two foreign communities, it will be readily understood
that there are but two chances for the future: the Negroes
and the whites must either wholly part or wholly mingle.[14]

In the twenty-first century we still have not decided, and
so the problem, in the absence of action, grows only more entrenched. Even as we voice support for equality and social justice, as our forebears did, four hundred years of building the
racial state continues to manifest itself in the form of segregated
neighborhoods, schools, workplaces, and daily lives.

In common with other societies, particularly those built in
the colonial era to include citizen and other, the shortcomings
of one generation become the challenges of the next. The treatment of Africans was clear "tyranny" in the fledgling center of
democracy, as de Tocqueville saw so clearly, the tragic flaw in a
society that still lacks the courage to mend it.

For too many people it has always been high-minded (often
performative) opposition to the flaw in the design rather than
grounded desire to overcome its prejudice that led them to support emancipation and then civil rights a hundred years later. It
was a matter of principle.

After so long, 150 years, it became nearly impossible for
them to see and embrace the actual people with whom they
always shared the land, conditioned as they were by the same

social forces as slaveholders. This, as much as anything else, is why the flaw would not merely damn the new democracy from being complete but also divide it for centuries.

To our nineteenth-century outsider there was a cautious optimism: "But in the picture I have just been describing there was something peculiarly touching: a bond of affection united oppressor with the oppressed, and the effort of Nature to bring them together rendered still more striking the immense distance placed between them by prejudice and law."[15]

Two hundred and fifty years after the Revolution, prejudice and law still warp the treatment of black America, the long half-life of a radioactive element that it shares with places like Brazil, South Africa, and India. Countries that were pillaged and intentionally half-made to serve a few at the expense of the whole, separate and unequal in public spaces as well as in the national imagination. And so we remain interdependent, unable to fully avoid each other. Unwilling to fully integrate.

If a consensus had emerged in Philadelphia to abolish slavery and integrate the newly freed, instead of a contractual compromise hewing to the colonial status quo of the time, a still uncalculated cost to the future would have been avoided. Like every generation ever after, the only thing known about the toll is that it would be high.

Instead, an increasingly uneasy union broke apart after eighty-six years—*I shudder for the future of my country*—exploding into one of the worst civil wars in all of history. It was the most dramatic price, some would say the ultimate, but even it does not capture the full scale of violence and anguish that have unfolded here. The South would lose that conflagration in the most devastating manner, yet, night for day, erect a series of monuments to its alternate view of itself and wish of history. The North would win but quickly forget the lessons of victory and dangers of compromise. Homespun terrorist organizations, such as the Ku Klux Klan, would become part of mainstream American politics into the twentieth century. Protests, riots, paralysis in the face of mass suffering, and a government so broken as to barely function would all plague the democracy built along the race line.

If they had known this would be the price paid, how many of the Founders would have refused the original compromise with slavery and held out for a better deal? Jefferson, I'd wager a nickel, would take another chance.

Or maybe, like politicians today, he would take what he could in his own time and leave the spiraling conflict for the future to solve. But those who live in that future, amid the accumulated wreckage, no longer have the right to say they don't know better.

3

FORGETTING AND REMEMBRANCE

It is man's salvation to forget no less than it is his salvation to remember. And it is wise even in the midst of the conflict to look back on those that are past and to prepare for the returning problems of the future.

—Walt Whitman, *Drum Taps*

In the summer of 1837 seventeen-year-old Benjamin Montgomery was sold from Loudoun County, Virginia, to a slave trader from Natchez, Mississippi. It was part of the cataclysmic second slave trade between the Old South, where the soil had been depleted, and the Deep South, where it was a boom time for cotton. The overseas slave trade had been abolished in Virginia more than forty years before Montgomery's birth because of a confluence of the humanist concerns underpinning the constitutional ban on transatlantic slavery and, whether by design or unforeseeable consequence, an increase in the domestic market. Virginians quickly came to understand their next fortune would not be in agriculture but, like some institutions you have heard of, in human flesh.[1]

Little is known of Montgomery's parents, but they would likely have been born in Virginia shortly after the Revolution. His grandparents were either saltwater Africans or born here in the generation before independence. Like nearly all African Americans today, Ben Montgomery's American roots stretched back to colonial times.[2]

We live in a moment increasingly aware of the abject violence of slavery and, at least in the abstract, its continued echo across the land. It began with a kidnapping, the victim separated forever from family and everything that was known, before a forced march to the coast. It continued through the four-thousand-mile-long savagery of the Middle Passage, where, as Olaudah Equiano, who was kidnapped as a child one afternoon when he and his sister were playing in front of their house in Iboland, wrote in the first widely embraced book by a black person in the English language, "The groans of the dying, rendered the whole a scene of horror almost inconceivable," and every attempt to resist was punished with a sadistic lashing. Any who could "threw himself overboard rather than endure any further."[3] The cruelty terminated in generations-long bondage and violently extracted labor. Better to die in the sea. Four hundred thousand survived and endured.

The violence from end to end was unspeakable and perfectly ordinary. Long before the Civil War the continent, as Jefferson accused King George, was awash in blood. Violence to the body was matched by violence against the spirit, extending from the clear brutality of chattel slavery to, as de Tocqueville depicts, the familial intimacy of master and slave. Abuse was not merely sanctioned by law and social custom; it happened every day at home.

Whites and blacks in eighteenth-century America often lived under the same roof, and the customs governing their interactions were a silent acknowledgment of how personal the relationships often were. After colonial labor laws were rewritten from a fixed term to perpetual bondage, people of the time spoke of slaves who had been "born in the family," whom one owed special consideration, and those who had not and could be used more roughly. Besides being a diabolical economic model, slavery was, in permanently linking the lives of individuals, anthropologically and often literally a form of kinship.

There were a host of unwritten, mutual expectations and agreements among those who had grown up together in the same household. Two of the most basic were that you never broke apart a family and that you never sold anyone who had been "born in the family." In these customs was a devastating admission that those who owned slaves knew perfectly well that they weren't dealing in property, as the law tried to claim, but in human life. Any fig leaves concealing the naked viciousness of slave owners and their enablers in the early country, however, were soon removed as the cotton trade began to create vast new wealth and America, already deeply materialistic at the time of revolution, grew even more so.

At its peak, America would produce three-quarters of the world's cotton supply. It was by far the country's largest export and one of the greatest sources of wealth in history.

The land would be reshaped as old-growth forests were

cleared to make way for vast plantations, often abandoned every decade as the soil was depleted. Ships would be built to take the cotton to market. Warehouses would be built to store it. Lawyers would be needed to write contracts; a sophisticated financial market, spanning the ocean, would be needed to supply capital; insurance agents would be needed to protect against loss. Mills would be constructed across New England to loom it. Ports built to carry it abroad. All in addition to the thriving inland market in slaves themselves. Cotton would turn the yeoman farmer ideal of the Revolution into a modern economy of industrial production and sophistication that would be perfectly recognizable to any financial professional of today. It is not an overstatement to say that the foundation of America as we know it was built on slavery and that slavery, of course, came from the blood of slaves. As the cotton market expanded into industrial agriculture in the Deep South, black people in America were sold downriver into an institution ever more brutal. Kingdoms and democracies alike depended on it.

In addition to the wealth being created in the Americas, cotton, like tobacco and sugar, constituted the hypotenuse of the triangular trade underpinning the British Empire. America may have left the empire, but it could never escape the trade.

In the years after Eli Whitney filed patents for his cotton gin, which revolutionized the efficiency of the crop, production of cotton grew fivefold, from 70,000 bales in 1830 to 2.85 million bales twenty years later. The number of slaves sold away from their families in the Upper South into the cotton belt grew proportionally, eventually reaching 3.2 million in 1850.[4]

The complex intimacy and competing value systems of antebellum America, with their kaleidoscopic spectrum of human, intellectual, and economic relationships, remain something of which America can barely speak from the shame of it all. Shame, we know better than our own hearts, is a feeling you will do anything in the world to hide.

Ben Montgomery was sold downriver at the beginning of this boom by a master near his own age with whom he had grown up. Whatever other family he may have had, he would never see any of them again.

Montgomery arrived at the Natchez Negro Market in the Mississippi Delta, in all probability after marching under armed guard, ten hours a day for three months, chained at the wrist to the man beside him and to a row, fore and aft, of as many as a hundred other men. In Natchez, we know, he was bought by a former lawyer in his early fifties named Joe Davis, the oldest of ten children from a Scots-Irish family that had followed the frontier from Georgia to Kentucky. Joe's dad was a Kentucky horseman and part-time tobacco farmer. From these modest beginnings Joe, who had only a rudimentary formal education followed by a short apprenticeship, had become a successful lawyer in one of the roughest parts of the country.[5] He would in time become one of the most successful cotton farmers in a state full of prosperous planters.

Ben, whom Davis bought that fall morning, would eventually become essential to his pursuits, managing all the plantation's business affairs, in addition to becoming a successful merchant in his own right. Joe was attracted to eighteenth-century utopianism and prided himself on being a man of technology and enlightened thought, who could tell himself he was such a successful, benevolent master even his most valued "laborer" was rich. He had perfected slavery in America. It was,

like a great many things about the institution, not simply peculiar but flat-out weird.

When they reached Hurricane that morning, Davis's five-
thousand-acre plantation, Montgomery took one look at the
setup and immediately headed for the hills, running away from
what he saw as a backwoods morass. When he was eventually
hunted down and recaptured in the unfamiliar swampland, Davis questioned him to find out what would make anyone run
away from Hurricane, which had a reputation as the model
plantation. Ben Montgomery, literate and accustomed to town
life in Virginia, according to oral history, told Davis he was too
good to be his slave. The two men then negotiated the understanding that Montgomery would be able to keep his own book
of whatever he was able to earn on his own, in exchange for la-
boring in Davis's fields.

Montgomery would soon learn surveying, which he did for
pay from other area landowners; became an adept mechanic;
filed patents for a propeller to power shallow-water vessels; and
set up and ran a local post office and a general store, selling
goods to the slaves and whites on the local plantations and river-
boat traffic on the Mississippi.

Besides his responsibilities at Hurricane, Montgomery had
broad oversight of the land that Joe Davis gave his younger
brother Jefferson, who, after Secession, became president of the
Confederacy. During the war, Montgomery would extend credit
to both Davis brothers and eventually buy the two properties,
some nine thousand acres, outright for the equivalent of eight
million in today's dollars. There he would found one of the
country's first black towns, increase its production, and eventually lose it all at the end of Reconstruction.

There have always been exceptional black people in America, and some of them found ways to thrive even within the strictures of slavery. According to historian Janet Hermann, the reason Montgomery never bought the lives of himself and his family was that there simply was no place in America at the time where a black man could be free.[6]

Joseph Davis is enshrined in Mississippi history as one of the founders of the state and a model slave owner, an oxymoron if one exists. He was no doubt an extraordinary man for his place and time. Montgomery, who scarcely exists in public record, was even more so. But slavery, which rested on claiming a Ben Montgomery couldn't exist even as it bent its rules to make allowance for and take advantage of exceptional individuals, had no intrinsic regard for human ability, only skin and opportunism. Just as gifted people in bondage in antiquity worked as teachers for the wealthy or administrators for the state, personal abilities were not seen as proof against the lies of race or the institution of slavery. Whatever one's abilities, they belonged to someone else.

Simply living in proximity and even forming close human relationships in structurally uneven space did nothing to alter devotion to slavery and racism. They were merely exceptions that flattered the ruling class. One may make, and even feel good about making, exceptions for the individual who has overcome gross inequality without relinquishing, and in fact reinforcing, inequality itself. The material and psychic inducements were too great. Those who practiced slavery convinced themselves oppression was a natural order, which they sat atop of by virtue. It held Joe Davis in esteem for his enlightened approach to the practice and held Ben Montgomery in bondage.

Devotion to the practice and the false pride it instilled had always been stronger than devotion to liberty or humanist values, which in minds so corrupted had never meant what it did to Adams or even Jefferson. After the Civil War the exploitation of slavery would continue to inform American capitalism. The view that one is naturally better or more deserving than others remains stubbornly with us, showing itself in individual vanity, spurious science, and policy. If Reconstruction had continued its course, we might already have achieved the aims of a free state. Instead, we remain in shadow of the Confederacy, holding on to the entrenched views of race even in a society that has moved on its surface closer together. The progress is real. It simply doesn't extend very deep.

As damning or ennobling as Americans today find the first third of their story, there is another yet more serpentine, tragic theory of the country's origins. It reveals a cynicism and corruption unique to large-scale slaveholders and their ability to manipulate the levers of politics and human relations, rooted deeply in the dynamics of power but not necessarily the people themselves.

In *Somerset v. Stewart*, a landmark case tried before the King's Court in London in 1772, the chief justice of the English legal system found in favor of a black man, Somerset, whose putative master, Stewart, had bought him in Boston, moved with him to London, and was at the time of the case attempting to dispatch him to the Caribbean to be sold. After Somerset was imprisoned aboard a ship bound for the West Indies, his English godparents (he had converted to Christianity in London) were scandalized by Stewart's conduct. They filed petition on Somerset's behalf, suing for his freedom. In his landmark decision,

William Murray, earl of Mansfield, ruled that English law did not support slavery.[7] Somerset was released.

The ruling did not take on the question of the colonies, but it freed thousands of enslaved blacks who lived in England and Wales at the time and buoyed hopes for abolition across the Atlantic, where revolution was still four years away. Inversely, the blow against the African trade stoked apprehension among slave owners in English America. The southern colonies, according to this view advanced by British historian Simon Schama among others, joined in the Revolution precisely so they might continue to practice slavery, free from the more forbidding laws of England. An act of Parliament, enforced by the Royal Navy, ended the transatlantic slave trade in 1807, a year ahead of the United States. A second act outlawed slavery in all English colonies in 1833, more than a generation before Americans did so in cataclysmic violence.[8]

In the nineteenth century, America was one country among many in the Atlantic world grappling with slavery, and it was far from the most progressive. In 1793 Canada became the first dominion in the British Empire to abolish slavery. Haiti would win its independence in 1804 after a successful war against France, striking fear in the hearts of mainland slave owners. The English Caribbean had been, at least legally, free for a generation by the time of the Emancipation Proclamation. America was, in fact, among the last countries on the Atlantic Rim to abolish slavery.

From inception, according to the less forgiving view, the American Republic was a souls-for-silver deal with the devil. *Dred Scott v. Sandford*, an 1857 Supreme Court ruling that essentially would have made slavery legal everywhere in America, was at last the line of slavery's aggression that liberals refused to countenance, but it was a line more compromised than anyplace else in the English-speaking world. This ruling robbed Americans of their claim of exceptionalism and condemned them in a manner contrary to what the most cherished myths in national life would have us believe. How you elect to read this past says a lot about your present circumstances.

In the *Dred Scott* decision, widely regarded as the most significant event leading to the Civil War, the US Supreme Court ruled that slaves who escaped or otherwise made their way into a free state must be returned to their masters. It was the opposite of what the English courts ruled in *Somerset*, and as Frederick Douglass, who was self-emancipated, would note, it "made the Negro everywhere a fugitive in his own country."[9]

Lincoln resigned himself to the inevitability of war, in the conviction, as the historian David Blight notes, that "only in the killing, and yet more killing if necessary, would come the rebirth—a new birth—of the freedoms that a republic makes possible."[10] It was more than two hundred years since the arrival of the *White Lion*.

The war that followed was meant as an assertion of core principles for a new nation that would defend them. This reason for war, as Blight notes, would be lost by the future, as the war was recast in false light: "When [Lincoln] said 'the world can never forget . . . what they did here,' . . . he envisioned an ideological struggle over the meaning of the war, a society's tortured effort to know the real character of the tragedy festering in the cold and in the stench of all those bodies awaiting burial. Lincoln seemed to see fitfully that the rebirth would be rooted in the challenge of human equality in a nation, ready or not, governed somehow by and for *all* the people."[11]

The Civil War's promise was not only ending once and for all the taint of slavery but crucially also integrating freedmen into society, which as Douglass would point out was the real task at hand after Lee surrendered at Appomattox and the last of the 620,000 dead were buried. It is a total number of dead roughly equal to those of all other wars in American history combined.

During the eight years immediately after the war, it felt as though the promise of America was well within reach. "The anti-slavery platform had performed its work," Douglass wrote soon after hostilities ended, "and my voice was no longer needed. . . . A man in that situation . . . has only to divest himself of the old, which is never easily done, but to adjust himself to the new."[12]

Even amid the euphoria there was an abiding reality that centuries of injustice would not be undone overnight. "An instant may snap the chain, but a century is not too much to obliterate the traces of former bondage," Douglass preached in an 1866 speech, a year after the Thirteenth Amendment was passed. The task at hand was doing exactly as he realized, obliterating the traces of former bondage. To do this would require maintaining the spirit of revolution "in a careful equilibrium against the dangers of both excess and disillusionment and inaction."[13] The fear of excess suggests an excitement at that moment for continued progress that seems difficult to square with the ensuing years.

Douglass, among the most prescient statesmen the country has ever produced, thought this could only be achieved through integration, which he articulated better than anyone at that point in time. It wasn't the war, but fully bringing the black population into the mainstream of America, that would fulfill the Revolution.

In the brief period after the Civil War known as Reconstruction, blacks occupied prominent positions in government, schools were funded to teach and train the newly freed in preparation for full participation in American life, entrepreneurs founded businesses, and African American artists rose to new prominence.

Douglass, who was recruited to run an undercapitalized bank lending to freedmen, believed, as Lincoln had come to believe, that it was the destiny of America to be a model of democracy regardless of race, gender, or class.

Nor did Douglass, Lincoln, or abolitionists of the time conceive of integration as simply assimilating African Americans into preexisting white norms, which were, after all, so shaped by bigotry. The future for African Americans was to be full participation in the material and moral life of American society. But it would be an America that they *had a hand in shaping* and in which they could see themselves:

> The nearest approach to justice to the negro for the past is to do him justice in the present. Throw open to him the doors of the schools, the factories, the workshops, and of all mechanical industries. For his own welfare, give him a chance to do whatever he can do well. If he fails then, let him fail! I can, however, assure you that he will not fail. Already has he proven it. As a soldier he proved it. He has since proved it by industry and sobriety and by the acquisition of knowledge and property. He is almost the only successful tiller of the soil of the South, and is fast becoming the owner of

land formerly owned by his old master and by the old master class. In a thousand instances has he verified my theory of self-made men. He well performed the task of making bricks without straw: now give him straw. Give him all the facilities for honest and successful livelihood, and in all honorable avocations receive him as a man among men.[14]

Blacks in America, whom Douglass called Anglo Africans, had contributed infinitely to the building of the country; their future, then, was to keep building for their own prosperity as well as for the country as a whole. Douglass has come to believe, like the founding generation, that America had a unique destiny. Moreover, he believed that as long as black people were oppressed, America would never achieve its proper greatness. Integration served not only black Americans; in this view, it was central to the idea of America itself. A hundred and fifty years later, the doors are still only partially open. We have yet to be fully received.

Even in defeat the South remained defiant of the racial strides made in the years after the war, and there arose a vehement, violent backlash from white southerners, led by former soldiers, who had lost the war but not relinquished the dream of white supremacy. They organized in terror squads such as the Red Dragons and Ku Klux Klan to suppress civil rights, a campaign that conservatives in the United States have yet to relinquish 150 years later.

If anything survives so long, there is a reason. In this case it is because their efforts were often effective. The first signs of northern capitulation arrived in 1877, when Rutherford Hayes, after an inconclusive election, agreed to stop enforcing the rights of blacks in the South in exchange for southern Democratic support in the Electoral College, which let him gain the White House.

Want for political expediency and raw power had triumphed over the desire for equal justice. As soon as federal troops were withdrawn, southern Democrats began to construct the system of Jim Crow that would keep them in power another eighty years. This happened not only with northern compromise but also with legal support.

The brief march toward integration was fully halted and reversed in a series of 1875 judicial rulings known as the Civil Rights Cases, which declared that most of the new freedoms awarded in the Thirteenth, Fourteenth, and Fifteenth Amendments were not enforceable. By means of political terror, and in the hearts of the people themselves, Americans born after the war slowly embraced revisionist histories in the name of putting the past behind. The sacrifice demanded by this new narrative nationhood was the black body.

After the federal government withdrew its troops as an appeasement to white southerners, Ben Montgomery would lose control of Davis Bend, which he had turned into the third-largest producer of cotton in Mississippi. His son Isaiah would eventually start the entire enterprise over again in the town of Mound Bayou, one of the first black towns in the country and a draw for luminaries as diverse as Booker T. Washington and Theodore Roosevelt, who saw it as the new model of black citizenship after the Civil War. In the ensuing years it would be the only place in the state blacks could still vote.[15]

Given a free hand, Ben Montgomery continued the utopian experiments he had witnessed growing up and created a democracy that he also prepared to defend. When asked how they were able to maintain their independence, Milton Crowe, a descendant of the town founders and its longtime local historian, replied, "They were well-armed. There was a Gatling gun on the roof of the bank."[16]

The terms of reunification, and the rise of the American empire in the following century, would lead to a new national myth of American greatness and further cast a pall on national understanding of the past.

In the following century, after American military might proved decisive in the Allied victory in World War II, the United States would be held up as the paradigm of democracy and leader of the free world, teaching by example what a democracy was.

This is the compromise that millions of whites, eager to avoid grappling with integrating black Americans, would embrace and that millions of new immigrants hungry for a new identity after the desperation of feudal Europe chose to learn. It is the compromise that defines us still four hundred years after the *White Lion* landed in Virginia.

4

THE LAND WITHOUT MEMORY

He was not a soldier and knew that he would either be killed or die of hardship and so not be present on that day when the South would realise that it was now paying the price for having erected its economic edifice not on the rock of stern morality but on the shifting sands of opportunism and moral brigandage.

Perhaps that is what went on, not in Henry's mind but in his soul. Because he never thought. He felt, and acted immediately. He knew loyalty and acted it, he knew pride and jealousy; he loved grieved and killed. . . .

—William Faulkner, *Absalom, Absalom!*

The second-greatest emblem of America at the end of the nineteenth century is Frédéric Bartholdi's Statue of Liberty, a gift from France to America, which was dedicated in 1886. Every schoolchild learns at least part of the poem the American poet Emma Lazarus wrote that is cast into the pedestal Liberty stands astride, which would welcome millions of new arrivals fleeing Europe. These were the tired, poor, huddled masses the new century would be concerned with, not the Negroes originally referred to by the broken chain and shackle at Liberty's feet. Even a 151-foot-tall symbol could be made to mean something else.

The greatest nineteenth-century American symbol is the Lincoln Memorial. By the time of the Gettysburg Address in 1863, nearly 250 years of degradation and racist slander against the intelligence, morality, and ability of blacks had accrued in North America. Entwined with the lies were white projections of their own behaviors and psychological fears: bulwarks to assert individual separateness from the cruelties of a slave-based society, as well as a self-conscious assertion of the superiority of a system so obviously broken it needed a coping mechanism. Frederick Douglass noted this well before the development of modern psychoanalysis:

> Few evils are less accessible to the force of reason, or more tenacious of life and power, than a long-standing prejudice. It is a moral disorder, which creates the conditions necessary to its own existence, and fortifies itself by refusing all contradiction. It paints a hateful picture according to its own diseased imagination, and distorts the features of the fancied original to suit the portrait. As those who believe in the visibility of ghosts can easily see them, so it is always easy to see repulsive qualities in those we despise and hate. . . . This is the white book of libel against me, and all who look like me. Still passed from generation to generation.[1]

As moral philosophy Douglass's statement is, of course, correct, and as psychoanalysis his critique is fifty years ahead of its time. The "disorder" he has diagnosed might well be a collective delusion, if the goal were truth or morality. But just as Christianity was altered in America to suit material ends, it is a disorder that refuses all logic because its interest is not truth or morality, outside of surface appearance, but power and need for self-justification. As such it is a perfect system. The fruits of the immorality and irrationality Douglass saw so clearly are beneficial. If blacks cannot be held in bondage forever, whites may still hold on to their childish fantasy of superiority, beneath that a fixation on animal desires—food, genitalia, power—in perpetuity.

After Lincoln's assassination in April 1865, six weeks into his second term, Andrew Johnson, the vice president, was sworn in. Johnson was an ill-educated senator from Tennessee, a slave state, who was a Unionist during the war and whom Lincoln chose as his running mate from political calculus. As president, Johnson opposed the Fourteenth Amendment and offered the southern states terms of reconstruction that would restore the old political order, including black codes. He was the first president to be impeached, surviving conviction by a single vote, foreshadowing the terms on which the country would in fact reconcile. The South's one immovable demand for peace was to be allowed to continue subjugating black people.

One hundred and fifty years later, the compromised terms of reunion continue to resonate eerily through a political landscape in which Republicans spread their message primarily through a right-wing media that radicalizes the white psyche. The institutional Left responds to it only reactively, in terms intended to split the difference, even as ethno-nationalists scream the presidential slogan "Make America Great Again" with gleeful rage. "This superstition of former greatness serves to fill out the shriveled sides of a meaningless race-pride which holds over after its power has vanished," Douglass observed.[2] The country's second chance after the Revolution to free itself, Reconstruction, was squandered.

In addition to the sentiments of white racist aggression and resentment that would remain bulwarks of American politics after the Civil War, the newly freed population faced the material challenges of access to education, employment, and housing. These are the concrete issues that would be central to the question of integration from the nineteenth century until the twenty-first century and which we still fight over as though that fight—at least the *terms* we must address—had not already been settled. A nation whose sovereignty rests in its people requires an educated citizenry. Blacks had been uniquely denied education as a tactic to subjugate them. Housing and labor were the other two principal areas of racial enforcement and unnatural harm. Four million citizens had had their wages stolen and had been forced to live without real shelter. They now faced the task all victims of disaster, be it natural or man-made, encounter: how to properly begin life again, in this case even as those who had terrorized them tried to control their future. The task was wisely understood and the proposed solution—forty acres and a mule—spoke directly to the problems.

Black Americans would actually receive no assistance at all. In fact, they were punished with a century-long denial of even the most basic rights for having the temerity to be living proof of the crimes their country committed against them. There is

no other example in history of one group of citizens treating another with this degree of malice *after* a war has ended. Where
else would those who had sued for peace ever have such power
over the putative victors?

The same irrationality and immorality that Douglass observed in the nineteenth century continue to hold sway in the
twenty-first century, a near-hysteria impervious to and contra-
dictory of reason, because of the accrued prejudice of generations that continues to regard black people as a caste apart to
whose problems the only logic applied is the logic of race.

It is a caste to whom, in the white mind, no social contract
is due and who may be shunned to an outer darkness of civic
life as part of an ongoing negotiation between whites of various
disposition over the appropriate amount of oppression that may
be tolerated—in housing, in education, in employment, in the
law—all the while screaming their good intentions.

The retrenchment and resistance to integration that arose
after the Civil War continue to dominate not only the material
and social worlds of America's citizenry but also the deep interior of the white self, which has always been constructed in
opposition to the black self. White Americans, North, South, in
the spreading West, in the new wave of European immigrants
soon inculcated, were at base unwilling to accept black Americans as their equal in every way, and that resistance shaped the
law. It shaped schools. It shaped cultural institutions. It shaped
cities and the land itself.

Immediately after the war, revisionist narratives based in
white southern resentment, coupled with former slave owners'
long-harbored fears of black retribution against them, quickly
emerged. Southerners did all they could to resist a fair and equal

society during those abundantly fertile years, preaching white supremacy, employing terrorism to suppress civil rights, and above all telling themselves that their loss during the war was only a temporary setback.

In all of this they were laying the foundation to continue resisting a state in which black and white were integrated into a single nation, a democracy based on equality. Instead they embraced a counterfactual mythology, which claimed that the war had never been about slavery at all, but states' rights, or preserving an imagined southern way of life in the face of northern aggression, memorializing the Confederacy and those who fought for it as heroic and just. Things that mark the landscape, as anyone who has spent time down south knows, unto this day.

As they mounted increasingly successful legal challenges to the newly enshrined rights of blacks, a system of Jim Crow segregation and debt bondage emerged that enforced the unequal status of the formerly bonded, which would persist as legal doctrine another hundred years and whose vestiges still illuminate contemporary politics and jurisprudence.

The South had always understood that even northerners opposed to slavery did not believe in black equality. They had tested the line to see how far they could go and found the answer was pretty far indeed, if still not as far as they wanted. When black rights were annihilated by the Supreme Court in the 1883 rulings known as the Civil Rights Cases, rendering the Civil Rights Act of 1875 illegal, Associate Justice John Harlan cast the sole dissenting vote in an opinion that was striking for its honesty about recent history and its prescience about the future:

Constitutional provisions, adopted in the interest of liberty and for the purpose of securing, through national legislation, if need be, rights inhering in a state of freedom and belonging to American citizenship have been so construed as to defeat the ends the people desired to accomplish, which they attempted to accomplish, and which they supposed they had accomplished by changes in their fundamental law. . . .

The Thirteenth Amendment, it is conceded, did something more than to prohibit slavery as an institution resting upon distinctions of race and upheld by positive law. My brethren admit that it established and decreed universal civil freedom throughout the United States. But did the freedom thus established involve nothing more than exemption from actual slavery? Was nothing more intended than to forbid one man from owning another as property? Was it the purpose of the nation simply to destroy the institution, and then remit the race, theretofore held in bondage, to the several States . . . ?

Harlan goes on to note the crucial distinction between merely granting the rights of freedom and actively honoring rights of citizenship: "That there are burdens and disabilities which constitute badges of slavery and servitude, and that the power to enforce by appropriate legislation the Thirteenth Amendment may be exerted by legislation of a direct and primary character for the eradication not simply of the institution, but of its badges and incidents, are propositions which ought to be deemed indisputable. They lie at the foundation of the Civil Rights Act of 1866."

Nor is there anything new, except another 150 years of evidence, in Harlan's critique of the hypocrisy of American conservatives when it comes to the power of the federal government and the centrality of race in national politics and jurisprudence:

> Congress, with the sanction of this court, passed the most stringent laws—operating directly and primarily upon States and their officers and agents, as well as upon individuals—in vindication of slavery and the right of the master, it may not now, by legislation of a like primary and direct character, guard, protect, and secure the freedom established, and the most essential right of the citizenship granted, by the constitutional amendments. With all respect for the opinion of others, I insist that the national legislature may, without transcending the limits of the Constitution, do for human liberty and the fundamental rights of American citizenship what it did, with the sanction of this court, for the protection of slavery and the rights of the masters of fugitive slaves. . . .

> Today it is the colored race which is denied, by corporations and individuals wielding public authority, rights fundamental in their freedom and citizenship. At some future time, it may be that some other race will fall under the ban of race discrimination. If the constitutional amendments be enforced according to the intent with which, as I conceive, they were adopted, there cannot be, in this republic, any class of human beings in practical subjection to another class with power in the latter to dole out to the former just such privileges as they may choose to grant. The supreme law of the land has decreed that no authority shall be exercised in this

country upon the basis of discrimination, in respect of civil
rights, against freemen and citizens because of their race,
color, or previous condition of servitude.[3]

Centuries of prejudice accrued in the white mind meant that
even after blacks won the legal rights of citizenship the custom of exclusion remained so deeply entrenched that the forces
of whiteness would fight to continue it in the courts and every
street in the country.

In the wake of this reversal blacks lost the protection of
the law, and political momentum shifted back to the forces of
white supremacy. The cause of equal justice would not move
significantly forward again until the 1950s. Significantly, it
would count as a major victory when public accommodations
were no longer segregated. Another way to view it, of course, is
that it took nearly a hundred years to regain the ground we lost
after the Civil War. The fact that the mid-twentieth-century
restoration of rights won in the nineteenth century counts as
a high-water mark in American history tells profoundly of the
depth of race hatred in America and how low the bar we have
set for progress is—where else on Earth would getting on a bus,
or going to lunch without having your head busted, be considered one of the nation's greatest moral victories? Maybe this is
the etymology of the expression "one step forward, two steps
back" that black people so often use to describe American politics, another way of saying four years forward and a hundred
years back. This isn't history. This is memory.

The points of view on the court that voted against equal
protection for America's newest citizens at the end of Reconstruction encompassed a broad political and regional spectrum.

Of the eight justices who voted against enforcing the civil rights of black people, three were from the border state of Ohio, two were from New York, one was from Massachusetts, one was from Kentucky, and one was from California. Harlan, the dissenter, was also a Kentuckian, who had supported the Union and supported slavery until after the war, when he had a reversal of mind. There were, notably, widespread public protests in the wake of the ruling, but there were not enough who believed in the humanity of African Americans and their rights as citizens to change the law.[4]

The larger willingness to accept and harbor white supremacy, or passively submit to a state that does, was an attitude that would mark liberalism for much of American history and on which more active forms of disenfranchisement depended.

In the same manner that northern delegates made compromise with their southern counterparts during the Constitutional Convention, for reasons of economic and military expediency, after the war it was easier to reintegrate those who had destroyed the country than to integrate black people. The duality between the speed of reunification and the resistance to black civil rights is as deep as it is persistent on the American right and, as we will see, would take countless forms as the nineteenth century bequeathed itself to the twentieth century.

From the beginning, Americans have subscribed to the belief we are a nation apart, born to a unique place in the world, especial in our virtues, and blessed in a fate that bends toward justice. The Revolution, after all, gave the United States pride of place as the first modern democracy, setting into practice the *theory* of democracy that had been gaining currency since the Enlightenment.

During the period in which democracy was first theorized, commerce was creating a class of wealthy, educated persons who did not belong to the aristocratic order, while reason was supplanting religion and two of its essential functions. The first religious function, explaining the mystery of the universe and humanity's place within it, was a function that science was rapidly disrupting. Religion also orients the individual toward society and his or her place within it. However, wealth and education emboldened the bourgeois to question the monarchy, whose claim to power was based on religion as much as any supporting pillar of power. As reason and the law spread, kings, with their special place atop the chain of being, became obsolete. Educated, informed people are, this argument goes, perfectly capable of ruling themselves.

The American Revolution was a revolt of the middle class. But by the time of war, the colonies had existed for 150 years as a monarchical dominion—an English colony among the constellation of overseas colonies that included Jamaica, Barbados, and the smaller Atlantic islands, as well as vast countries such as India, Nigeria, Kenya, and South Africa. It had much in common with them.

In all of these places wealth was transferred from colony to mother country, and the labor and land of the people were coerced. It was a tripartite system of subjugation and genocide, which included the strategies of cultural genocide and assimilation, practiced in Australia; the direct and indirect rule that followed the conquest of India and Africa; and the slavery practiced throughout the Americas, in which people were moved from one part of the system to the other.

The US practiced them all, seizing the lands of the Native Americans by force and removing them from it, attempting to assimilate them where possible, and shipping Africans to the New World to supply labor. Unable to subdue the indigenous nations into assimilation, the English set about to destroy them. Eventually, under the leadership of Andrew Jackson, Native Americans were corralled into the reservations that remain a feature of the country. And under Jim Crow it would treat its black citizens as colonial subjects to be exploited and administered.

Democracy, founded in equality and enlightened reason, and colonialism, founded in racism and self-justifying solipsism, are the ruling and rising signs that have steered the US ever since. This complex system called the United States has always been a multicultural space. It is the relationship of its different peoples to the state that has always been the problem.

Societies, as adjacent areas in the humanities and social sciences remind us, invest in belief systems that affirm who they are. This is equally true of religious belief systems and social ones. Or, as the ancient priests of Yoruba put it, "The gods didn't make man. Man made the gods."

Race in its completeness, its pervasiveness, its willful suspension of disbelief is the paramount god in American life, affirming superiority over others and organizing our cities, our churches, our dinner parties, our conversation with ourselves—driving the internal narrative, each over the other. It is so complete a system that we accept its contradictions to the point of fighting a war to end slavery, while still subscribing to racist beliefs. We shame those perceived as racist while enthusiastically participating in schools, businesses, churches, and newsrooms so morphed that we tell ourselves we are neutral participants in meritocracy.

Integration is not only a material but an existential threat to this balance because it not only alters the fabric of our lives and the rules we learned to play by; it shatters the gods of race and, by asking who we think we are, challenges the self.

Black exclusion from democratic citizenship is the backdrop against which millions of immigrants were flocking to a rapidly expanding America. In the late nineteenth century they were lured by its promise of freedom and escape from crop blight and famine in Scandinavia and Ireland. In the early twentieth century a wave of Eastern and Southern Europeans arrived: Jews and Italians fleeing hunger, feudalism, and virulent anti-Semitism. Soon a new layer of white self-understanding was added atop the original base of Native Americans, Africans, indigenous Mexicans, Chinese, Dutch, German, and other Protestant Northern Europeans, above all the English.

The largest groups of newcomers were the four million Italians who immigrated between 1870 and 1914, followed by more than two million Jews, arriving first as political exiles from Germany, which after centuries of growing tolerance (beginning with the Napoleonic emancipation in 1806) had grown increasingly repressive toward its Jewish citizens. This blood hatred culminated in the populist *Völkisch* political movement, whose core assertion, after years of evidence to the contrary, was that Jews, unlike Poles or Slavs or Italians or any other of the myriad ethnic groups in greater Germany, were a race apart that could never be integrated into society, one of the libels near the root of it all. This first wave of approximately 250,000 German Jews was followed in the early twentieth century by nearly two million Central and Eastern Europeans fleeing poverty and pogroms.[5]

In America the continent was too large, its population too diverse, the fear of others too great, the need for labor too pressing, to make any such claims. Despised as any of the groups may have been in Europe, in America the same people were afforded the right to vote and to participate in society the moment they were naturalized. Only the colored were held apart, an apartness that would prove perversely useful as the country grappled with the question of how to integrate so many newcomers, who swelled the overall population by nearly 10 percent.

Assimilating this largely destitute immigrant population, unfamiliar as they were with English, let alone American norms, was not merely a matter of not discriminating against them—in the way that blacks were then being relegated to separate train cars, neighborhoods, and classrooms—it was a set of active measures, centered primarily around housing and education, to inculcate in them the skills, behaviors, and beliefs of their new society.[6]

A great deal of the effort focused as well on public space, where a sense of community was fostered among those from so many different communities in a new cultural commons taking shape. This civic effort centered not only around work but also the leisure activities that united all Americans, no matter their station. As historian David Nasaw observes in *Going Out*,

> Racial segregation and racist parody were not invented by turn-of-the-century showmen. They became constituent elements in commercial amusements because they were already endemic in the larger society and because they provided a

heterogeneous white audience with a unifying point of reference and visible and constant reminders of its privileged status.

"White" immigrants and ethnics who dressed appropriately, acted decently, and had the price of admission were welcomed inside. . . . As Henry James discovered in 1904 on his return to the United States . . . the "aliens" were everywhere being rapidly Americanized or, as he put it, magically lifted to a new "level," "glazed . . . over . . . by a huge white-washing brush."[7]

Not only were African Americans excluded from this sphere—in segregated baseball teams or in a boxing ring where the ascent of a Jack Johnson as heavyweight champion set off a frenzied search for a new "great white hope," a term still embedded in the language—excluding them was the mechanism by which whiteness was taught. The ridicule of blacks and the spread of racist stereotypes were often the *point* of an evening's entertainment, like spreading the gospel is the point of a mission. The new myth of whiteness was created, like the old myth, in opposition to the alleged inferiority of blacks.

Blackface images that dominated the American cultural landscape from the stage were ubiquitous, serving as the most primitive of symbols to demean colored people and to convince white Americans that they were *both* a malevolent force in need of control and a docile group of intellectually and morally inferior people deserving of the ridicule, in need of control. The goal was to extend an invitation to a new generation of whiteness while also teaching the depths of hatred reserved for those outside this social community. Tellingly, these images, which would be a common feature of American entertainment through the early days of television and continue in various mutations in the early twenty-first century, began in the years leading up to the Civil War as southern propaganda.

As motion pictures grew as a vehicle of mass entertainment and artistic expression, they closely mirrored the growth of modern America. One might easily argue that aside from jazz, which is a blending of European and African musical sensibilities, film, which is a mash-up of technology, P. T. Barnum spectacle, and storytelling both visual and narrative, is the most American of all art forms. Certainly, few other forms have been so integral to shaping how Americans see themselves and how the world sees Americans.

Tragically, from the beginning, a generation after the Civil War, African Americans were reduced in the new medium to stereotypes borrowed from vaudeville, the reigning entertainment form in the antebellum era. The most notorious example was, of course, *Birth of a Nation*, the story of white vigilante justice after the fantasized rape of a southern woman by a black man, but even Thomas Edison's peep-show company featured such fare as "The Pickaninnies Doing a Dance."[8]

As these entertainments grew into cultural institutions, they formed a common ground, transmitting the attitudes of segregation and a national mythology of white supremacy, buttressed by the racist caricatures seen everywhere from the Broadway stage to the box of cereal one ate in the morning. This new culture granted access to a shared language of Americanness, helping immigrants master its codes and share in a bounty from which blacks were excluded.

This would be fortified in the material realm by an exclusionary promise of upward mobility, as the new immigrants were afforded the rights of citizens, and with such rights, public policies meant to ensure them access to secure housing, education, and meaningful livelihoods.

As the United States assumed new prominence on the global stage, this was the domestic landscape from which the myth of the American Century grew. It is from this point in time that most Americans would like to think the story begins, long after the original sin. But sin by then was everywhere, commercialized as modern media and entertainment. Racial attitudes could now be transmitted at global scale, generation to generation, in public as well as in private, where they ever remain a currency of politics, ready for anyone to draw from. But these attitudes also shaped culture and customs in ways that most still do not discern.

If they think about it at all, they believe it to be heritage, or natural, because it has been conditioned at the level of instinct.

5

AMERICAN EMPIRE: FROM PERIPHERY TO CENTER

Maturity of mind: this needs history, and the consciousness of history. Consciousness of history cannot be fully
awake, except where there is other history than the history of the poet's own people: we need this in order to
see our own place in history.

—T. S. Eliot, "What Is a Classic?"

This is where the story begins to turn, gets stuck, and refuses. The reason it cannot alter course is because of what
we know and are not willing to know about ourselves and the
world. At each rupture that opened the possibility of mend-
ing the wound of race in America, the country balked, giving
her white citizens a new deal and a sense of themselves as just,
while giving her black citizens half a hope. The injury of race, to
the individual, to society, to the human enterprise, was not one
injury—slavery—as we fervently wish to believe. Nor was it a

single historical act, abolished and castigated to the past. It is a
dozen large acts played out on a global scale and an uncountable
galaxy of smaller ones—those committed, active as violence,
passive as a lie, every day in an American lifetime—multiplied
by the number of people who have ever lived in America. This
is what it means to say that each of us creates history. It is upon
this that our world is built, and ourselves, too.

Besides being visible in the material conditions, the relative
wealth, of each racial group, the primacy of race is ever present
in the stories we tell ourselves about who we are, what our country is, and how things work in the world, as well as our place
within the constellation of all the Americans who have ever
existed.

That is why the story gets stuck here, because who would
not like to live in a universe in which our story of ourselves is the
center of all things, irrefutable and true?

National myths are all about holding their people up big
and strong. They whisper your magnificence in triumph and
times of doubt, reminding you who you are in the truest part of
yourself, which no one but your own people can see. The myth
we tell across America, of course always half the tale. But who
did Americans in the early twentieth century believe themselves
to be? What was their hidden truth?

Hard work and individualism have always been fetishized
in America, and the myth of democracy America exports to the
world, but this is when the myth of the immigrant was added
to it. In this version of the national myth, the members of the
first new generation arrive poor, sacrifice, and labor with nothing but their own hands. Their children enter the respectable

professions and save. The third generation is free to pursue its creative desires. The hardworking, honest individual triumphs in ways that only the lazy are denied, if not all at once, at least in the fullness of time.

The real story is more complex. A great deal of necessary light has recently been cast on this enduring myth of individual agency versus federal policy in the success of the American middle class, as if poor people do not work hard. The idea that you can succeed in the face of hardship obscures the reality that official policy has had a massive impact on who has succeeded and how, which is what the policy was designed to do, and its goal was to ensure security for white America.

The new awareness has come about primarily through renewed examinations of the carceral state by writers like Michelle Alexander and Caleb Smith, and the attention that Ta-Nehisi Coates and Richard Rothstein have drawn to the ways the Federal Housing Authority tipped the real estate market to enrich white over black through practices like redlining: refusing to make mortgage loans to African Americans or in neighborhoods where black Americans lived. Together these two practices would both incarcerate black Americans at a wildly disproportionate rate—beginning almost immediately after the Civil War and continuing through the present. They would further exclude black families from participation in the greatest expansion of middle-class wealth in American history, while ensuring residential segregation. In the past as well as the present, Americans turned a willfully blind eye to these discrepancies, only to enact a theater of white awakening to injustice, or white outrage that anything they do might be called unjust,

whenever the public evidence became too overwhelming to ignore. Even after "awakening" to the problem, as we have over
the past five years, calls to remedy it are muted.

As the national housing market collapsed and the nation reeled
from unemployment during the Great Depression, President
Franklin Roosevelt initiated some of the most progressive legislation in American history. These programs included Social Security, which provided a safety net for millions. A century later
the American Right remains opposed to these programs despite
their proven efficacy. In any other context, solutions that worked
well would have been applied universally. In the United States,
official policy was akin to giving everyone a vaccine against cancer on the condition that no one share it with black people.

Guaranteeing home loans, which would allow millions of
Americans the security and economic benefits of ownership,
was only one New Deal initiative that was discriminatory by
design, or in the ways it was applied. This compromise with racism was necessary to secure wide enough political support even
as the stock market collapsed and blizzards of dirt were raining
down in the heartland. The FHA, whose guidelines contained
the now notorious provisions to exclude "inharmonious racial or
nationality groups" from "infiltrat[ing]" white areas, in order to
protect government investment and that of white home owners,
was simply one of the more blatant discriminations.[1]

There was no evidence up until that point to suggest that
the presence of African Americans affected home values. Writing it into lending guidelines made it so. It was a simple example of the race prejudice common to all white Americans of the

time, whether the most progressive New Dealer or sociopathic conservative. The white book of libel was a shared inheritance, helping European immigrants make peace with each other across what might otherwise be unbridgeable political and social divides. These new policies not only affected economic opportunities; they also shaped geographic segregation, education, and job access, for decades to come.

The pattern of de jure housing segregation created by the US government persisted until the Fair Housing Act of 1968. The patterns of de facto segregation have extended well beyond. The material effects of the original exclusion from the New Deal remain powerfully visible across America and are especially pronounced in great twentieth-century cities such as Chicago, New York, and Los Angeles, where the government actually *built* segregated housing for workers during World War II. The psychological effects remain as well and can be witnessed in the ways that American cities are currently re-segregating in the twenty-first-century process called gentrification, which is merely the same problem and psychology in reverse.

Although the Fair Housing Act, one of the three central tenets of civil rights in the twentieth century, abolished legal sanction for segregation, it remains largely unenforced. Many whites, whatever their party affiliation, do not view housing desegregation as inherently desirable, other than as an abstraction or token of diversity. Just as the nation rewrote the history of the Civil War and let collapse the goals of the Second Republic, allowing the most repressive parts of the southern agenda to determine the course of the peace, so too would a formidable backlash ensue after the historic victories of the 1960s, when even Republicans like Richard Nixon understood that more had to be done.

Whites had been taught by official policy during the New Deal, as well as ancient custom, not to live next door to black people. It was not easily undone. Former vice president Walter Mondale, who as a senator was one of the authors of the 1960s Civil Rights Acts, which restored the rights that were stripped from African Americans in 1875, recently wrote a newspaper editorial describing the ongoing state of segregation in the United States: "We know that growing up in an integrated community provides children with a better chance. . . . This is the story of the first 50 years of the Fair Housing Act: gradual progress and frequent setbacks. If the law's drafters could have been accused of anything, it was excessive optimism about how easily an integrated society could be unified. . . . But even as the epochal events surrounding their passage fade from collective memory, the Fair Housing Act persists. It remains a bulwark for advocates of justice and equality, as they advance inch by inch, toward a fairer, more integrated society."[2] This is the law the Trump family was prosecuted for breaking when it excluded African Americans from its middle-income apartment houses as late as the 1980s.[3]

The primary reason Roosevelt originally excluded blacks from so much of the New Deal, which lifted so many Americans, was to appease southern Democrats, with whom northern liberals had been in political alliance since Rutherford Hayes sold out Reconstruction. It is hard to overestimate the permanent damage this did, not only in withdrawing federal troops from the defeated South but also in signaling liberal priorities. This form of "working across the aisles" would long continue. This is the alliance former vice president Joe Biden joined in the 1970s when he worked with southern segregationists to limit the impact of school desegregation. Biden was not a rogue operator. He, like the Clintons, was an exemplar of the twentieth-century liberal party. The rationale has always been political realism.[4]

Power loves to conserve itself. Curtailing African American liberty and opportunity has always been a price liberals were willing to pay for their own position and comfort, so long as they had a cover story providing plausible deniability. The fig leaf has always been a version of the same formula, a claim that bolder measures are not politically feasible, making it possible to take comfort in the comparison between liberal "good intentions" and overt conservative racism. This ongoing progressive compromise holds the progress of black America hostage to the agenda of right-wing neo-Confederates, instead of enshrining it as the proper but unfinished goal of American democracy since the Revolution: "Nothing is more certainly written in the book of fate than that these people are to be free." Compromise afterward was never with history, not if you subscribe to reason, but with the histrionics of whiteness.

During the New Deal, Eleanor Roosevelt became the emblem of centrist good intentions, inviting to the White House Walter White, then chairman of the NAACP (a direct successor of the abolitionist movement), and the presidents of the nation's historically black colleges, which were originally built to educate the newly freed.[5] It was a canny political calculus between the establishment Left and spokespersons of black respectability, defining an alliance against both an increasingly Marxist Left, which was then seeking common cause between the black and white proletariat, and an unrepentant Jim Crow South.

In addition to creating the formula that the centrist Left would deploy throughout the twentieth century, it was also good political theater and would become a liberal ritual whenever subsequent White Houses wished to signify liberal solidarity with civil rights, while also bowing to the fear that more meaningful action was too steep a climb. This meeting helped allow President Roosevelt to claim solidarity with African Americans while also enabling the center Left to decouple meaningful action in the theater of race from the rest of its agenda. It afforded liberal whites the benefits of a racist state as well as the moral vanity of claiming to be against it.

By all measures Roosevelt was the most progressive president of the twentieth century, but "Roosevelt's record on civil rights was modest at best. Instead of using New Deal programs to promote civil rights, the administration consistently bowed to discrimination. In order to pass major New Deal legislation, Roosevelt needed the support of southern Democrats. Time and time again, he backed away from equal rights to avoid antagonizing southern whites."[6]

Redlining was only one of many exceptions to programs created in the years between the Great Depression and the post–World War II period to greatly aid white American freedom from "fear and want" while excluding Americans of African descent in ways still visible in their public effects and obvious in their material outcomes. Unlike our friend Richard West in seventeenth-century Virginia, who opined, "Yet I cannot see why one Freeman should be used worse than another merely upon account of his complexion," Americans were moving toward a state in which, like the shackles at Liberty's feet, they could no longer even acknowledge the difference because it harmed an emerging new myth of American exceptionalism and the American Dream. This induced myopia remains under-acknowledged.

During the New Deal the National Recovery Agency (NRA), to cite another far-reaching example, not only offered whites the first crack at jobs but also authorized separate and lower pay scales for blacks. Among other things, the NRA effected this by setting a minimum wage and maximum cap on the number of hours that a worker could be required to labor. Blacks, excluded from both provisions, would be overworked and underpaid.

This injurious asymmetry was present as well in the Social Security Act, which secured for most Americans a retirement fund, but excluded the 40 percent of African Americans who labored in the agricultural or domestic industries, the most common occupations for blacks in the South at the time.[7] All of this was by design. Any whites who suffered, and many did, were simply collateral damage. The intention was to harm black people.

Equally telling, Roosevelt withheld his support from an anti-lynching bill and a bill to abolish the poll tax, two of the preferred methods of white southern terrorism. Once again, "Roosevelt feared that conservative southern Democrats, who had seniority in Congress and controlled many committee chairmanships, would block his other bills if he tried to fight them on the race question."[8] Left and Right could only find accommodation if blacks were sacrificed.

As the American Dream expanded around them and the government demonstrated an incredible ability to better the lives of its citizens, African Americans, largely excluded from the New Deal, nevertheless maintained a sense of hope. They had been effectively shut out of politics since the collapse of Reconstruction and now had their first perceived ally since Grant, even if much of the allegiance was simply symbolic. Symbols have meaning. They also began to organize with increasing sophistication to pressure Washington politicians.

Despite the unreliability of their liberal partners, it was, according to Mary McLeod Bethune, seen by many as "the first time in their history" that African Americans felt that they could communicate their grievances to their government with the "expectancy of sympathetic understanding and interpretation."[9]

The glimmer that shone with the promise of a better future was in reality more sympathy than substance. But in fairness, not all programs were equally exclusionary. The Works Progress Administration employed approximately 350,000 African Americans. The Civilian Conservation Corps saw black participation total more than 350,000 by the time the program was shut down in 1942. In 1934 the Public Works Administration (PWA) had inserted a clause in all government construction contracts that established a quota for hiring black laborers based on the 1930 labor census. As a consequence, a significant number of blacks received skilled employment on PWA projects, but they were the exception. These early examples proved the efficacy of active measures, but even as they benefited the rest of America and reshaped the country, black people were largely left out for no better reason than sheer southern spite and northern capitulation.

Important pressure to improve race relations during this period came not only from home but also from international scrutiny as the nation approached World War II, in which more than one million African American men served in a segregated army.[10]

The African American community was only too well aware of the hypocrisy between what America said it believed, as it went off to fight German, Italian, and Japanese aggression and illiberalism, and how it treated a large swath of its citizens— even if the official government position was to deny there was discrimination against blacks in America. The response to this duality was well captured by the *Pittsburgh Courier*, then the nation's largest black newspaper, which launched a "Double V" campaign, urging its readers to fight the battle against Nazis abroad and inequality at home, against the element in American life that had more in common with Nazis than with the revolution of 1776.

It was in this climate that A. Philip Randolph and Bayard Rustin, the leading race men of their day, persuaded Roosevelt to ban discrimination in the defense industry, threatening a march on Washington if he did not. In the face of such a potentially embarrassing event, Roosevelt signed an executive order declaring that "there shall be no discrimination in the employment of workers in defense industries or government because of race, creed, color, or national origin."[11] This victory would be followed by a presidential order from Truman in 1948 that integrated the segregated armed forces, making the military the first institution in America to do so.

The military, however, was also the nexus of one of the largest exclusions of blacks from the new wealth of America. The G.I. Bill, introduced to provide financial support for the more than sixteen million soldiers returning from World War II, included cash stipends for education, low-interest mortgages, job-skills training, low-interest loans, and unemployment benefits. It was unevenly administered, to say the least. Most of the one million African Americans who served in World War II never saw any such benefits from what former president Clinton would one day describe as "the best deal ever made by Uncle Sam."[12]

What was true in the Union states was even truer in the former slave states, where Jim Crow excluded black students from "white" schools, and as a result, historically black colleges, many founded during Reconstruction to educate freedmen, struggled to respond to the rise in demand from returning veterans. After World War II, black Americans who wished to attend college in the South were restricted to about a hundred public and private schools.

As Ira Katznelson documents in *When Affirmative Action Was White*, those exclusions were by no means limited to the former slave states or to education. Katznelson reveals how the G.I. Bill, like Social Security, housing loans, a minimum wage, and fair working conditions, was deliberately designed to accommodate Jim Crow laws, declaring it was "as though the GI Bill had been earmarked 'For White Veterans Only.'"[13] As he notes elsewhere about national policies that were consistently warped by the racist intent of the South, amid northern passivity, "It was a classic example of how intense factions can win when the majority is indifferent."[14]

As the postwar order was being built, black veterans had no access to it. Brandon Weber notes that "in 1947, some 70,000 African American veterans were unable to obtain admission to crowded, under-resourced black colleges. The University of Pennsylvania—one of the least-discriminatory schools at the time—enrolled only 40 African American students in its 1946 student body of 9,000."[15] As a proportion, that rounds to 0 percent.

As with the original New Deal, housing was also an area of redoubled disparity: "The G.I. bill included support for banks to provide veterans low-cost, zero down-payment home loans across the United States. But of the first 67,000 mortgages secured by the G.I. Bill for returning veterans in New York and northern New Jersey alone, fewer than 100 were taken out by non-whites."[16] These twin efforts lifted millions of American families into the middle-class American Dream, while further reinforcing the norms and prejudices of whiteness.

Although the G.I. Bill helped whites advance, it was often used to ignore blacks and put returning soldiers back in their place: "The G.I. Bill helped place 6,500 former soldiers in Mississippi on nonfarm jobs by fall of 1947, but while 86 percent of the skilled and semiskilled jobs were filled by whites, 92 percent of the unskilled ones were filled by blacks."[17] It is another of the many ways the country actively constructed an apartheid state long after slavery had gone.

As the century wore on, millions of whites streamed into segregated suburbs, financed by Uncle Sam, where they were educated in segregated schools before going off to segregated universities, where they were prepared for a segregated workforce. In the evening they returned home to watch "Pickaninnies Doing a Dance," or *Birth of a Nation*, or *Steamboat Willie*, or else two worlds of culture in which, like the one outside their front doors, there simply were no black people. *They* had been erased by the magic of entertainment and housing codes, freeways, and railway tracks. *They* had been corralled into ghettos out of sight, except for the twinkle of Uncle Ben's smile. Alternately, one might have gone to see a segregated baseball game or a minstrel show, or rooted for a great white hope who could beat Jack Johnson, or repeated like a catechism any of the lies about black inferiority that were and remain so commonplace in American life. ("They are lazy and violent, and if they cannot succeed, it is because they do not deserve it.")

The effect remains fundamentally etched in national politics. The alliance between northern liberals and conservative southern Democrats held until Lyndon Johnson muscled through the Civil Rights Act of 1964. In protest, many southern Democrats, led by Strom Thurmond of South Carolina, one of the most antidemocratic states at the time of the Revolution, left the Democratic coalition to support Barry Goldwater, the Republican presidential nominee. Thurmond, who secretly had a child with a black woman who worked for his family, was a fixture in the US Senate until 2004 and one of the staunchest voices against integration.

Goldwater's primary attraction for Thurmond and others was that he had made resistance to civil rights one of the pillars of modern Republicanism, writing it into the party's official platform, where it has remained in coded form ever since. To be conservative in America has always meant to support, be it actively or passively as liberals, the segregationist order that defined the past.

The cautious need to "go slow," on the other hand, has endured in liberal America since the eighteenth-century notion that slavery should be abolished gradually. It is an appeasement of the racist point of view. Appeasement simply means to make peace on the enemy's terms. These are the terms that have ossified in the liberal establishment since the Great Depression. Liberals no longer need active resistance from conservatives; they have so internalized the idea of "going slow" that they have been going slow since Lincoln was killed, instead of waging war to complete the revolution.

In the middle of this period of stuckness, however, the US Army, heeding the pressure of African American activists, was forced to integrate and did so successfully. Although one might debate the wars America entered in the name of manifest destiny in the nineteenth century or in the name of empire in the second half of the twentieth century, and the cynical way black bodies became cannon fodder in Vietnam, serving in the US Army was long viewed across the political spectrum as noble. Its success in integration over the ensuing years would be studied by numerous industries seeking to do the same in the later part of the twentieth century, as the country made the first earnest attempt at desegregation and racial equality since the Second Revolution.

It should come as no surprise that one of the first institutions to commit to desegregation should contain lessons for all the rest. Just as a clear commitment to segregation continues to plague the country's cities, a true effort at integration in the military seventy years ago has resulted in an institution that, while imperfect, is widely viewed as one of the more integrated places in the country. At the same time, the commitment to segregation in housing, education, and employment gives us cities and schools that are overwhelmingly unequal and divided instruments of the racist agenda, and the concomitant differences in wealth and educational attainment that are a goal, not a product, of segregation.

When national turmoil erupted a generation later, finally forcing America to act on civil rights, it was the result of the greatest mobilization of private citizens in the country's history. The resultant backlash, in the final third of the twentieth century, would see the Left return to the old formula of southern appeasement.

Ongoing segregation, accompanied by liberal as well as conservative denial, means we still find it all but impossible to give voice to the issues of integration in the twenty-first century. The simple reason is that while political rhetoric may seem more enlightened—words like *diversity* and *multiculturalism* really come with a silent qualifier: *a little, some, enough*—beneath it the historical liberal racism, which has forever joined white interests across the political spectrum, remains the same.

The new euphemism of "white privilege," like other forms of what sociologist Karen Fields calls "racecraft," is a semantic shuffling meant to signify its speaker as aware of the problem, and wishing to distance herself from it, but far from committed to fixing it.[18] Like so much else when it comes to the problems created by race, we still use language like a fig leaf to cloak not simply what is really going on but also to mask a personal reluctance to act.

6

THE DEATH OF THE CIVIL RIGHTS MOVEMENT

The Dutch cut the Achilles tendon of a slave escaping for the first time, and who makes a second try gets the right leg amputated; yet there is no way to stop the spreading plague of freedom.

—Eduardo Galeano, *Faces and Masks: Memory of Fire*

The philosophers have only *interpreted* the world, in various ways. The point, however, is to *change* it.

—Karl Marx, *Theses on Feuerbach*

How long shall they kill our prophets?

—Robert Nesta Marley, "Redemption Song"

I don't remember how old I was the first time my uncle decided it was time for my cousin Christian and me to see the old neighborhood, where my grandparents lived when they first moved to Chicago from Mississippi. Christian is a year younger, and we must have been seven and eight. Nine and ten at most. I know this not because of any definite marker of time but because of its effects. We were young enough that it made a formative impression, more welt than bruise, more preconscious than memory.

My uncle, the only surviving male on my mother's side of the family, had told our parents he was taking us to the park to practice swimming, as I remember, before driving the two of us to Maxwell Street for beef hot dogs draped with pickles, doused in relish, anointed with mustard. Christian slathered his with ketchup, which I always thought was disgusting, but Chicagoans are opinionated about hot dogs. Every neighborhood boasts a place that claims to have the best in the entire city, and my uncle went on about why a hot dog that wasn't from Maxwell Street should be legally required to change its name. Like all the food of memory, nothing else will ever taste the same.

At the time, decades before the area was gentrified, Maxwell Street was still one of the main commercial corridors of the Westside. The neighborhood had once been a ghetto that housed poor Irish immigrants, then Italian immigrants, then Jews from Eastern Europe, before becoming a ghetto to house poor black people coming north to escape Jim Crow, as the Southside neighborhoods where they were originally confined overflowed. It would eventually become predominantly Mexican American and then succumb to "redevelopment." Unlike many neighborhoods pocked by segregation, that part of town had always been a ghetto, and it was one of the vibrant parts of a bustling city. The inhabitants had changed, but everyone in the area still called it Jewtown. It was a different ghetto, but the hot dogs, Polish sausages, and Italian beef were all still kosher, set amid a devil's bazaar of flea markets, pawnshops, juke joints, and every imaginable kind of church. Whoever they were, the people of Maxwell Street always needed money and salvation or maybe just succor.

Chris and I understood it was not a place our parents wanted us to be, making the trip all the more thrilling and sweet. My uncle had separated us from our mothers, from our fathers, from our younger siblings because he wanted us to know where that side of our family started from. He did not say this to us at the time. We were only boys. But as each of my maternal cousins reached prepubescence, he or she would join us in the car for a trip to the old neighborhood. It wasn't a place we had ever lived—there was nothing sentimental or nostalgic about the trips—but it was part of where we were from.

The hot dogs came wrapped in yellow wax paper, bundled with hand-cut fries dripping enough grease to seep through this first layer of packaging, the white butcher's paper surrounding it, and stain the brown paper bag that held the whole bounty. We would divide it all in the car and start munching as my uncle drove us around, pointing out the landmarks he remembered from when he was a boy. As the years passed, it became a ritual, continuing no matter how far we moved away.

The last station on this pilgrimage was always the same, the ritual repetition driving the lesson further home, deeper and deeper into the interior. We would head down an ominous block of run-down houses, the ghetto in the heart of the ghetto, on Monroe Street, where the car would stop abruptly in front of an abandoned two-flat. No matter how many times we took the trip he would say the same thing, year over year, like a school principal who has a single lesson he wants you to know above all else before you matriculate into the world. This is only the palest of reasons I will always love him, as I picture him repeating, "That's where they killed Fred Hampton."

During the civil rights years many people were martyred. Martin Luther King Jr. was a great man, and Malcolm X was a great man. Angela Davis, one of the few women whose names we know from a movement that depended heavily on women, was great, and even greater for surviving. But in my family, which in all other matters believed in a politics of respectability, we were always partial to Fred Hampton. When we celebrate Dr. King's birthday, of course, there is a silent cenotaph holding space for the rest, because most of them, like Hampton, would today still be considered too radical for the mainstream, especially as the sixties gave way to the present and the fight for gross rights on the southern front turned into a more subtle battle for wholeness.

Where the 1950s civil rights movement harkened back to the Emancipation Proclamation, reminding Americans they had reneged on central tenets of the contract, the later civil rights movement pointed toward the Revolution, telling the world whether or not we were free was no longer the question, but the full measure of that liberty, which by definition included self-determined.

Fred Hampton was murdered at the hands of local law enforcement, in league with federal authorities—it sounds like conspiracy, but it is fact—in an attack so gruesome the bullets tore apart the walls and doors of the apartment where he lived, leaving blood and body parts scattered like debris, as though a man was a thing no more substantial than Sheetrock.

To tell the truth, I didn't fully understand—in fact, I didn't understand at all—why my uncle was telling us anything so frightening. I also didn't know the cause of Hampton's death was still a contested matter: the official version was the black men inside the apartment had opened fire on the innocent white police. The truth is Fred Hampton was sleeping. The truth is at twenty-one he was of an age when most men today would be buying their first beer, graduating college, all of life ahead. He was my uncle's age, but he would never take his boys for a joyride to get hot dogs. Fred Hampton at twenty-one was a man—black, brilliant, charismatic, ethical as they come—whom the United States government and its people feared.

When I was a kid, the conspiracy to cover up his murder would not be legally proven for another twenty years. For black America it was accepted and settled fact. It's become popular of late for white people on conservative news shows to dabble in conspiracy theories, but black people are the ones who live them.

It was only recently, as an adult, that I fully understood why my uncle took us to an old crime scene that was by then fading, as the seventies turned to the Reagan years, even from black consciousness. He wanted us to understand things about who we were and where we came from that even our parents could not tell us. Hoping as they must have been that these were not things we would need to know.

The Black Power movement was the fiery outgrowth of the civil rights movement's nonviolent phase. It was a direct response to the vicious attacks of local government and private citizens against black America's peaceful protest of racial brutality.

By the time of King's assassination, many blacks in the North and on the West Coast had come to feel his agenda was too modest, speaking to an agrarian past of the Jim Crow South, not the economic oppression of the industrial economy and the new ghettos that ensnared them.

Across the North, segregation took the form of exclusion from the federally guaranteed mortgages that fueled the growth of the suburbs, jacked-up rents in slums because its audience was captive, kids packed into inferior schools, and policing with untold hidden menace instead of vigilante mobs that everyone could see.

Segregation had learned, in an age of mass media, to be more subtle, working out of sight in station houses, courts, businesses, and hidden social understanding. In the North, racial brutality worked by the combination of policy and prejudice, not just the shotgun. But, as in the agrarian economy, the Pinkertonesque intention, like the armed guards used to suppress workers' rights, was to exploit black labor—now in factories instead of fields—without affording the black worker the full benefits of citizenship.

Where much of the moral language of the early movement was indebted to religion, the largest congregations of American Christianity, Methodists and Baptists, had always refused to speak out against slavery. The southern branches of both churches remained silent, and the northern branches issued the mildest of rebukes. The language of Christianity would never be enough to battle the hardened white supremacy of America because Americans had been told directly and indirectly that God was on their side. They had co-opted even the prophets. The new phase of the movement had come to understand that moral suasion, the public language of black protest since the abolitionist movement, was not enough. The new movement was no longer quoting the Book of Isaiah but looking instead for other gods and laying claim to science in the form of Marx's critique of political economy and Frantz Fanon's clinical analysis of colonialism, connecting their struggle to the larger global fights against oppression.

At the same time, America as a whole was rapidly moving from the periphery to the center of power, in the process holding itself out to the world as the exemplar of a free state. The civil rights movement not only undermined American authority to do so; it was an unintentional embarrassment, showing that the leader of the free world was no less oppressive toward its black citizens than the European empires had been toward their peasants and colonial subjects. It was, as many observers noted, a country in no position to preach to others, built as it was on slavery and continuing injustice.

Over the course of the civil rights movement its language had shifted steadily from the Christianity of King, to the Islam of Malcolm X, to the purely secular language of the Panthers. Even before Malcolm Little joined the reactionary Nation of Islam, and even before Martin Luther King Jr. was killed, many were debating the utility of pacifist resistance. After Malcolm was killed, after Martin was killed, after Medgar Evers was killed, all hell broke loose. The summers of 1968 and 1969 saw mass uprisings in every major city in America. The police responded with violence, shooting dissenters, busting heads, filling hospitals and prisons.

After the fires, people were no longer calling simply for desegregation. The limits of rhetoric had been crossed. They were in the street fighting for what white Americans and the US government feared would become full-blown revolution. It almost did.

King and earlier civil rights advocates, such as Randolph and Rustin, had taught people the power of mass mobilization. Malcolm had taught black America a language of self-determination. The Panthers took it to the street and pulled the entire national political conversation to the left, with the effect of making less radical liberal goals more achievable. In the same way, conservative extremism would pull the early twenty-first century radically toward the right after the election of a black president, which must have felt to many of them like their own political death.

In the wake of the murders of King and Shabazz (after Malcolm changed his name for the second and final time), federal authorities feared "the rise of a messiah-like figure" who could unify the fractured elements of the civil rights movement. Twenty-one-year-old Hampton, bright, charismatic, and self-assured with a demeanor of baby-faced, near-beatific, innocence, was the man they feared.

Hampton dispensed with the language of the church and respectable statesmanship for a homespun oratory people related to. As a rising star, guileless and beguiling, or the man who once introduced Huey Newton to a rapturous crowd as "the baddest motherfucker I know," Hampton spoke the black English of the ghetto, not the pulpit, with all its fearless irreverence, profound emotional nuance, and plainspoken power, elevating it to the field of national politics. When Malcolm spoke, people heard someone of discipline and principle they admired. When Martin spoke, people heard the authority of a black Christ figure. When Fred spoke, kids on the street heard themselves.

The Black Panthers also furthered the strategy, going back to Du Bois and Richard Wright, of connecting the struggle for justice in America with the struggles for justice around the world. As nations in Africa, Asia, and the Caribbean threw off the yoke of European rule, the Panthers saw the black American revolt as part of a worldwide effort by peoples of color.

The Panthers were no longer simply demanding desegregation but questioning American power and America's way of making money. To them, integration was both impossible and undesirable without confronting America's role in the world and the role of capital in America. J. Edgar Hoover's FBI and local police forces infiltrated their ranks, sowed dissent, and committed extrajudicial murder (as distinct from the legal murder of the death penalty and the kind that happens every day).

The far reaches of the political Left, arguably the traditional ideas of liberalism, were systematically annihilated and with them a language, commitment, and organizing machinery for systemic change we have yet to fully recover.[1] In America it is white people who have a monopoly on violence.

The FBI had, since 1956, run a counterintelligence program called COINTELPRO, aimed at disrupting domestic political operations on the left. Among the groups deemed a threat were socialists, anti–Vietnam War organizers, and the civil rights movement. The Panthers were all of the above.

Even before they walked onto the floor of the California legislature brandishing rifles and shotguns, lobbying for their right to bear arms, the threat they posed to white power was existential. It led the black Left, and with it much of the American Left, to an unnatural demise, underscoring the fact that as recently as fifty years ago the status quo of the United States government was willing to use deadly force to suppress political speech on the left. It was as chilling as it was effective.

It was this violent resistance of local, state, and federal governments to Martin Luther King's nonviolence doctrine, meted out in every corner of this country, that radicalized the younger members of that movement in the first place. The violence deployed against the Panthers was not as immediately apparent as police batons and water cannons (to cite only the abuse that was broadcast, and so irrefutable), but it was just as effective, demonstrating that resistance to black power was not simply rogue southern sheriffs and vigilante mobs. It was national policy.

Whiteness and blackness are not static opposites, as the crudest understandings would have us believe. Rather they are (dialectically) entwined concepts and conditions. Whiteness wishes to reserve for itself the power to arbitrate the meanings of both whiteness and blackness, each of which has a range of values. But whatever the *shifting* meanings and relationship, whiteness *requires* blackness (a priori) in order to define itself. Equally crucial: all states described within the system are actually composed of two components. The first part is the actual thing or condition under consideration. The second component is its symbolic representation (the words, images, and social poses we use to describe it). The symbols sometimes mirror and sometimes distort (positively or negatively) the true underlying condition.

What made black power so threatening was not the leather jackets and military drills, but that it offered one of the very few possible paths out of race's labyrinth: by wresting from whiteness the power to define what blackness means, it undermined and threatened to unravel the foundational principle of the system of white control.

The definition of the white self may change across time and beliefs, but it always exists in relation to blackness and the power to define that relationship. Without blackness, and power over blackness, whiteness becomes a null set. It has no value. Both individual and society must look elsewhere for a philosophy of being. Just as a nation defining itself as leader of the free, home of the brave, was revealed to the world as a racial state, indebted to the social and economic practices of the British Empire and European colonialism (of which it was both product and producer), so were a people who regarded themselves as educated, well-to-do, civilized, indeed the rightful heirs and stewards of "civilization" appalled by the brutality of force deployed on behalf of whiteness: purple-faced adults spitting at children exercising their right to an education. If one was not truly appalled, the idea of oneself as civilized required that one perform indignation. Or at the least sympathy. The distinction between real belief and performance does not matter so long as the acts under scrutiny are visible and public. When they are private and deniable, as private thoughts always are, the difference matters a great deal.

American whiteness, with its new role in the world, and new pretentions, had an image problem. The problem for those who believed in justice was authentic: how to alter the racial state. For others, it was how to maintain white supremacy without being seen as a pariah in a world where the new watchword was freedom. Lynchings and water cannons were too much. Ghettos, exploited workers, prisons, and social death were acceptable. Appearing racist was verboten under the new codes of whiteness, but not racism itself.

The great resiliency of white supremacy owes in part to the fact that it is an interlocking tripartite system. Legal segregation and vigilantism constitute the first, most active component, manifest in the form of group actions like lynching in which entire towns would gather to picnic and watch the brutal executions of blacks, afterward trading souvenirs in the form of postcards and body parts. There is still an underground collector's market for such artifacts. But also individual acts of violence like mass shootings, or so-called stand-your-ground laws. Rituals in which the other is sacrificed to the god of whiteness, the destruction of the individual body a symbol and prayer for white dominance, usually under the guise of communal "safety." Law is order.

The other two pieces of the system operate more covertly, often requiring nothing more than passive deference to social norms. On an institutional level, as Stokely Carmichael and Charles V. Hamilton write in *Black Power*, a critique that rings as true today as it did in 1967,

> When white terrorists bomb a black church and kill five black children, that is an act of individual racism, widely deplored by most segments of the society. . . . But it is the institutional racism that keeps black people locked in dilapidated slum tenements. The society pretends it does not know of the latter situation, or is in fact incapable of doing anything meaningful about it. Institutional racism relies on the active and pervasive operation of anti-black attitudes and practices. . . . "Respectable" individuals can absolve themselves from individual blame: they would never plant a bomb in a church; they would never stone a black family. But they continue to support political officials and institutions that would and do perpetuate institutionally racist policies. Thus acts of overt individual racism may not typify the society, but institutional racism does—with the support of covert, individual attitudes of racism. Black people are legal citizens with the same legal rights as other citizens. Yet they stand as colonial

subjects in relation to white society. . . . This is not to say
that every single white American consciously oppresses black
people. He does not need to. Institutional racism has been
maintained deliberately by the power structure and through
indifference, inertia and lack of courage on the part of white
masses.[2]

In such a system, if one does not actively opt out and oppose it,
one permits it by default.

The third aspect of this system is internal: the under-
acknowledged forces that prevent white Americans from admitting such tacit support and their own passive role, let alone
confronting it. According to Robin DiAngelo, "White people
are sensationally, histrionically bad at discussing racism." In
White Fragility, her best-selling 2018 book about race and the
white psyche, she goes on to observe the following:

> Like waves on sand, their reactions form predictable patterns:
> they will insist that they "were taught to treat everyone the
> same," that they are "color-blind," that they "don't care if you
> are pink, purple, or polka-dotted." They will point to friends
> and family members of color, a history of civil-rights activ-
> ism, or a more "salient" issue, such as class or gender. They
> will shout and bluster. They will cry. In short it is an unbe-
> lieving defensiveness that white people deploy whenever their
> ideas about race and racism are challenged—and particularly
> when they feel themselves implicated in white supremacy.

She argues astutely that our largely segregated society is set up
to insulate whites from racial discomfort, so they fall to pieces
at the first application of stress: "Racial hierarchies tell white

people that they are entitled to 'peace and deference,' they lack the 'racial stamina' to engage in difficult conversations. This leads them to respond to 'racial triggers' with 'emotions such as anger, fear and guilt . . . and behaviors such as argumentation, silence, and withdrawal from the stress-inducing situation.'"[3]

"Even a minimum amount of racial stress becomes intolerable, triggering a range of defensive moves. These moves include the outward display of emotions such as anger, fear, and guilt, and behaviors such as argumentation, silence, and leaving the stress-inducing situation. These behaviors, in turn, function to reinstate white racial equilibrium" and maintain racial dominance.

Moreover, "whites consistently choose and enjoy racial segregation. Living, working, and playing in racial segregation is unremarkable as long as it is not named or made explicitly intentional." However, when it is named, "Whites who position themselves as liberal often opt to protect what they perceive as their moral reputations, rather than recognize or change their participation in systems of inequity and domination." It is a liberal defense mechanism that holds race in its place.[4]

This slipperiness is near the core of the system yet is protected by so many other layers it is the least effective to address; however, it is perfectly comfortable to discuss, especially once you understand that by discussing it your own reputation is protected, and that nothing more is required. As an academic, DiAngelo is part of a field known as whiteness studies, a segregated response to black studies and critical race theory. It is by its own definition a form of fragility, to the extent that it centers a white narrative in the conversation about race. It is both aware and unaware of the ways it has absorbed, even appropriated, and displaced more radical black critiques of material racism (as well as troubling subject/object problems of the observer in the social sciences) to attend to the needs of the "progressive" white self.

Moreover, white studies operates apart from the scrutiny to which it might be subject in the more rigorous disciplines in the humanities and social sciences of which it is a subset. As a field it has absorbed a scintilla of the civil rights critique but has found a clever workaround in which the white ego is still paramount. It is not a solution to the problems of race but an illustration of how sophisticated and resilient they are.

Such performances of racial awakening have been a constant since the antebellum era. They also exemplify how talking about race and racism is a far cry from forty acres and a mule, or as the Panthers demanded, land, bread, housing, education, clothing, justice, and peace.

The brilliance of race as a technology of oppression is that even to be progressive does not mean to be committed to deconstructing the racial state. It is enough to modify the *performance* of whiteness, in this case a variation of the white savior with different desires operating apart, not in partnership, to maintain the centrality of whiteness.

The Civil War generation waged a blood battle against slavery because it came to understand only war could keep the South from slavery. The civil rights generation practiced civil disobedience en masse, registered voters, and sued the state for concrete, systemic equality, not partial, symbolic ones. As race morphs and hides, like a virus inside the psyche and political speech, it requires practical focus on the material substance of inequality, not simply symbolic performances, which often mask at least as much as they reveal.

The resiliency of institutional racism and the incredible number of strategies that individuals deploy to absolve themselves of responsibility at the sites where race functions led the Panthers to renew the call of mass collective action. As Hampton and the Panthers realized, that meant active and tangible demands. The pain of race is difficult to discuss and easy to dismiss. The anger of race is frightening. The competing shame of profiting from a system that oppresses others, and pride in being part of the institutions that provide a sense of security, are the crux of the liberal compromise: accepting any easing of the conditions that have stolen the rights of others as progress that soothes the national conscience but allows the core conditions of racism to continue. Or, as Malcolm famously said, "If you stick a knife in my back nine inches and pull it out six inches, there's no progress. If you pull it all the way out that's not progress. Progress is healing the wound that the blow made."

You can't police the American psychic interior, however, whatever skin is wrapped around it. What you can do is use institutional levers to heal the wound at scale. How many of the companies hiring race consultants, to cite one area of society, have equal hiring, mentoring, and promotion practices (not goals)? Is diversity a token effort in the form of a few visible hires, working on "diverse" projects (too often a form of marginalization), or something everyone in the global marketplace is expected to master? There exists a massive body of literature about what works and what does not in fostering a more integrated workplace, educational environment, or neighborhood. Sitting around talking, as in any endeavor, may help define goals, but it is powerless to execute them.

Without concrete action the audience leaves this theater, night after night, generation after generation, with the false comfort of being categorized as white in an apartheid state while telling themselves they are moral and good, or simply realists, but doing little to further tangible goals of equality.

In business as in politics, what has been added to the comfort of whiteness, after the civil rights movement was shot in its sleep, is the vanity of demonstrating one's bona fides as a supporter of racial justice. This performance is culturally inculcated. By demonstrating awareness or wokeness, one is demonstrating a badge of belonging, that you are a member of a group that cares about such things and went to a school or read a book or were raised in a milieu that taught you genteel behaviors and buzzwords. Yet any change to the existing structure is perceived as a threat because the system has also taught that blackness represents a unique threat, so you repeat your jargon from safe within the institutions and geography of whiteness. Integration threatens any self that takes whiteness as its most salient identity (without knowing it) across political lines, because it addresses the material, not the symbolic.

Talk, however, does have a role to play in solving the problem. At its best, it is meant to awaken our consciousness as a precursor to action. Such action is what J. Edgar Hoover feared (like generations of people invested in maintaining the status quo before and after) when he issued the directive to "prevent the rise of a 'messiah' who could unify and electrify the militant Black Nationalist movement. Malcolm X might have been such a 'messiah'. . . . Martin Luther King, Stokely Carmichael, and [Nation of Islam leader] Elijah Muhammed [*sic*] all aspire to this position. . . . King could be a very real contender for this position should he abandon his supposed 'obedience' to 'white, liberal doctrines' (nonviolence)."[5] The Panthers had witnessed what power does to truth and reached the same conclusion Hoover did, responding to the racial state in its own language.

When the Chicago police killed twenty-one-year-old Fred Hampton, this is what they were protecting against. Whites are so fearful of the call for real justice that their fear provokes not merely histrionic behavior but also well-thought-out acts of violence.

This is why the advocates of true justice and not merely symbols of hope continue to face an uphill battle. They are calling for change that whites do not want. Not really. The center merely asks us to stand by the compromise that Rutherford Hayes made, in which northern liberals stay in their place, passively aligned with southern racists. So while one of the major parties is always actively opposed to civil rights, the other party is passively opposed, flying low under the banner of political realism but really concerned only with the preservation of its own power. Or else they really are realists and measures of liberty is all the United States is ready for.

If such people had been in Philadelphia in 1774, there would never have been a Revolution. Civil rights and integration are the unfinished business of that Revolution, and the Panthers were made in its image, which is why the forces that prevented emancipation from happening in the eighteenth century were the same forces against civil rights in the twentieth century, which is what we are really talking about today.

The Black Power phase of civil rights arrived after the violence that whites directed at nonviolent organization by blacks in the

South but also because of impatience at the rate of progress in the country toward liberty. The measure northern liberals would apply to themselves has always been in relationship to the barbarism of the South—right-wing militias, with their implicit threat of violence against a just state—or extremists abroad. It has never been in relationship to the standards of democracy qua democracy, as it should be.

In 1966 the Black Panther Party for Self Defense put forth a ten-point program "demanding the overdue debt of forty acres and a mule . . . promised 100 years ago as restitution for slave labor and mass murder of black people." The platform continued to address a combination of economic, education, penal, and political concerns summarized in the final article: "We want land, bread, housing, education, clothing, justice and peace."[6] Where the previous generation of civil rights leaders were primarily focused on desegregation and equal legal rights that had been stripped in 1883, the Black Power stage of the movement zeroed in on the material legacy of the racial state, which has yet to be fully addressed.

Two of the articles might best be read as symbolic: the call for a military exemption and demand for full employment in the black community. The military exemption was aimed primarily at drawing attention to the fact that black men made up a disproportionate number of the dead in the disastrous war in Vietnam, and it sought to make clear the common cause they felt with those in Asia, Africa, South America, and the Caribbean struggling to rid themselves of imperialism. Full employment is a complex goal of Keynesian economics that dates back to the Great Depression. It might best be seen in practical terms as a call for increased investment, worker training, and job creation.

The Panther cri de coeur is symbolic on another level as well. King had delivered his famous "I Have a Dream" speech three years earlier, on the one-hundredth anniversary of the Emancipation Proclamation. The official name of the occasion was the "March on Washington for Jobs and Freedom." In taking up part of the older movement's agenda and pushing it further, the Panthers were signaling continuity with the past, as well as a new direction. The next phase of civil rights would be forged from the fire of the last. But the furnace was hotter.

This is the moment in the nation's history in which integration came into widespread parlance, but it was still only partially defined, because resistance to tangible actions like school busing and fair housing was so widespread. Politicians, like their constituents, learned the theater and rhetoric of justice as they worked ostensibly to "change the system from the inside." We have scarcely talked about it since, except in moments of crisis, which those in power understand will always pass when the surface conflagration subsides. In the system's normal state, which includes extremist legal attacks on the tangible outcomes of the last phase of civil rights, a prison complex of industrial-scale resegregation, and vastly unequal outcomes, the only thing we consistently protest is the complexity of our own entanglement and the depth of our complicity.

Part II
THE COLD CIVIL WAR

Traditions were crumbling, tolerance was seeping through the cracks. The walls of segregation were first breached in Berlin, where more than one or two "exceptional" Jews were now permitted to assimilate and live, like Mendelssohn, in two worlds.

—Amos Elon, *The Pity of It All*

Throughout history, the powers of single black men flash here and there like falling stars, and die sometimes before the world has rightly gauged their brightness.

—W. E. B. Du Bois, *The Souls of Black Folk*

When we say something has cooled, we simply mean it has gone from a state of high energy to low. At the unseen level its molecules have slowed down. When things cease to move at all, or just barely, we generally say they are frozen. When a substance or system goes from one state to another, this is called a phase shift. One of the curious things they always tell you to remember is that a phase shift, from solid to liquid, or liquid to solid, like water to ice, happens at the same temperature. So at exactly 32 degrees water is both freezing and thawing. It is in equilibrium, as the nation was when the numbers of slave and free states were the same. This is one way to think about the state of civil rights after the boiling heat of the 1960s.

At the dawn of the Second Republic it was widely understood that the success or failure of racial equality was the success of the Civil War itself. But the backlash of the Confederacy that managed to sweep the country into a new iteration of the racial state, instead of forward and nearer to freedom, was swift, brutal, and unbowed. The North won the war. The South won the peace. It was a counterrevolution in which de jure slavery was illegal but racial oppression was otherwise the law and custom of the land.

With its new prominence after World War II came a growing mandate for the US to serve as a global role model for democracy. This, coupled with the strategic brilliance of the civil rights movement, led to a series of rapid changes. A key tactic of the civil rights movement, in fact, was making sure the world saw what race in America truly looked like: the material depredation that had produced a third-world nation inside the world's wealthiest state. The political violence that the state used to continue it. These were things that could be filmed and photographed and sent out over the airwaves across the country and around the world.

This third iteration of revolution was the largest mobilization of citizens in American history. A phase shift was occurring. It was viciously suppressed as its leaders, like Lincoln before them, were assassinated: Evers, Shabazz, King, Hampton, one after the other. There were also endless challenges to the new civil rights legislation in courts, as there were in the Civil Rights Act of 1875. As I write this, in the early twenty-first century, those legal challenges continue.

The goals and movement toward integration were frozen where the mid-twentieth century had defined them, largely in terms of desegregation, the fight against the way things were. The laws no longer prevented you from going to school, or sitting where you liked, or living as you wished, but the deeper forces that prevented integration remained. You could live where you wanted as long as you could afford it, and some people could. The same might be said of schools. You could even make a lot of money. The caveat, of course, is you did it as an individual. As a group the system was frozen against you. If you triumphed, it was because you climbed over ice.

The system would point to these individual triumphs, or to these individuals themselves, as proof that enough had changed that the fight for equality was done, using symbolic individual victories to mask the abandonment of the black masses.

The active measures of affirmative action, which had been at the forefront of real integration, were met with a new wave of mass white resistance. Like many of the rules and customs that govern a society, they were largely hidden.

In recent decades, as new waves of immigrants arrived in America and globalization accelerated, the frozen state of civil rights persists beneath a surface of what is now termed diversity, in which an Asian man from Stanford, a Latina from Duke, and an African American from Princeton are all hired by the same multinational firm and pointed to as proof that the past is behind us. Or else the new arrivals are used as a multicultural shield to mask the lack of progress in solving the original problem and desire of white power. This has resulted in an increasingly slow rate of change, often for those deemed exceptional or acceptable or a model to white society. But the rate of mass change reached its apogee in the 1960s. The system then stopped thawing.

We are still suffering from the failure to reconcile our private and public selves, or our symbols and the truth, both of which hinge on what we perform, as opposed to the way things really are. Who we profess to be in public and who we are in private are often altogether different. Each of these selves is informed by its own necessities and desires. Abroad, America might promenade across the world stage in new finery. At home, it continues to savage nonwhites. It is an ancient moral truth that when doing right is intimate with the desire to be seen as doing right, rather than deeper commitment, it is only righteous by half.

Eager as we all may be to move beyond the past, we ignore the core goals of the civil rights movement—what's more, we began ignoring them almost immediately—and so have arrested progress at twentieth-century levels. At the same time, the backlash on the right grows ever stronger and more sophisticated in terms of judicial challenges to active measures like affirmative action and voting rights, a renewed political organization in the form of data-based gerrymandering, subterfuge at the federal agency level out of reach of public oversight, and savvier political speech ferrying the same old hatred.

On the left it has meant celebrating the symbolism of the exceptional, political speech that claims to be post-racial, signifying tolerance while feeling apathy and fear, and performing, generation over generation, the same rituals of awakening that have always damned liberals as unreliable allies.

The symbols are progressive, but white desire has always functioned the same across political lines. Both work together to keep us from moving forward the rest of the way. After the fire of mass protest cooled and the late twentieth century became the early twenty-first century, a modicum of integration for a few (the more visible the better), wrapped in a series of symbolic public gestures, coded speech, morally relativist political compromises, and punitive scapegoating, would be the force to maintain fin de siècle white equilibrium. When the system tried to move further into the future, the Right would respond with its most constant modes of resistance: intimidation and violence.

7

AFFIRMATIVE ACTION, DIVERSITY, AND SYMBOLISM

Culture is a sort of theater where various political and ideological causes engage one another. Far from being a placid realm of Apollonian gentility, culture can even be a battleground on which causes expose themselves to the light of day and contend with one another, making it apparent that . . . students who are taught to read their national classics before they read others are expected to appreciate and belong loyally, often uncritically to their nations and cultures.

—Edward Said, *Culture and Imperialism*

One of my homegirls left her job as an administrator at a prestigious university to take a position at the College Board, the 120-year-old organization that administers the SAT, among other tests, which serves as gatekeeper to higher education for the majority of American students. A few months into her new job a group of us met to unwind and catch up.

It was early June, and we were seated at a sidewalk café eating tapas, laughing to have such fine company, but she was unable to relax because of the stress of her new job. At work she was part of a group charged with rewriting the SAT to eliminate cultural bias. It was a thankless task, and the stakes—changing something that so many were invested in—were high. As it turned out, many people in her office, especially the people of color, actually despised the SAT because they understood better than anyone else that instead of leveling the playing field, it was actually extremely effective at reproducing existing social structures.

It is well documented that standardized testing, including IQ tests, measures only the dimensions of intelligence it has been crafted (wittingly or unwittingly embedded) to capture. Outcomes are greatly influenced by income. Those who can afford it buy extra help but also share the same underlying cultural assumptions as the test makers. If your grandparents were poor or immigrants to America, it is almost certain your IQ is measurably higher than theirs were.[1] It's doubtful you are any smarter. I know that I am not. You've been acculturated and given advantages money and access afford. The tests are most useful when comparing those of like circumstances. In education in America these circumstances are a direct reflection of parental income and education and, of course, how you are schooled, which is itself a function of money and, even more importantly, race. It's a classic catch-22. My friend, who is as smart as anyone in the country, had a chance to help fix it. She was stressed. Equally intelligent people had tried to fix it before.

The federally mandated integration of schools led to widespread white mobilization on a scale that is hard to appreciate or over-state, including a stream of lawsuits—the first in 1974—that continue to this day. Even most liberals, who believe in integra-tion as a theory, usually turn bitter with worry that their own fates and those of their children might be affected, their sup-posed places usurped by putatively less worthy African Amer-icans who did not live "in district" or score as well on the tests (implicitly accepting a society in which a quality education has been allowed to become an artificially scarce commodity).[2] Given all the effort invested in protecting the status quo, blacks who do manage to find seats at the most selective schools are still the exception, achieving similar results despite their coun-try's utmost efforts to stack the odds against them.[3]

I was reminded of this conversation while reading a re-cent newspaper article reporting that of the 895 seats at a well-regarded New York City magnet school, seven spots had been awarded to black kids.[4] New York schools are obnoxiously seg-regated, but these dismal numbers stood out. They also led to a lot of hand-wringing about the problems with segregated schools and unequal access to test-prep services (which result in a nearly 10 percent gain on SAT tests). There was briefly talk of aban-doning the tests, but in the end the city decided to keep things as they are. If you are a racist, you believe there is something wrong with black kids and that such unequal results make perfect sense. If you believe the world is a dog-eat-dog affair and it does not matter what the system is (so long as you and yours have a seat at the table), you will have no problem with the policy. If you believe in democracy, the Enlightenment, and social contracts, then it will seem to you that something is fundamentally wrong.

In most of the country, schools are funded by local taxes, which in turn results in unevenly allotted educational resources. New York City spreads *official* resources evenly. However, schools in wealthy districts enjoy a gray budget from parental gifts, which bring in as much as $1.4 million per school compared to a city-wide average of $1,000.[5] Furthermore, the educational system, like many basic services, was reconfigured under Rudolph Giuliani in order to attract as many suburban transplants as possible. The proliferation of so-called magnet or gifted programs was a result. So was the introduction of the tests-only approach for the most coveted spots. Giuliani knew, just like my friend at the College Board, that the tests are proxies not for intelligence but for something else.

When we talk about universal education, in such well-meaning initiatives as No Child Left Behind, we do not talk about equalizing the allocation of resources—let alone investing more heavily where investment is needed most or integrating those historically excluded from the system. We persist along the path that reinforces social discrimination even when presented with empirical data that tell us "increasing the social mix within schools appears to boost performance of disadvantaged students without any apparent negative effects on overall performance."[6]

Integration is objectively one of the easiest ways to impact outcomes. According to Rucker Johnson, a professor of public policy at UC–Berkeley,

> School desegregation and related policies are commonly misperceived as failed social engineering that shuffled children around for many years, with no real benefit. The truth is

that significant efforts to integrate schools occurred only for about 15 years, and peaked in 1988. In this period, we witnessed the greatest racial convergence of achievement gaps, educational attainment, earnings and health status . . . and this improvement did not come at the expense of whites.

Moreover, the longer students were exposed to integration and strong school funding, the better their outcomes in adulthood. This was true for children of all races. The beneficial effects were found not just for the children who attended desegregated schools, but for their children as well. School integration didn't fail. The only failure is that we stopped pursuing it and allowed the reign of segregation to return.[7]

Instead of pursuing policy that works, we simply deploy more testing to measure what does not.

In the same way public education came to be a proxy for local conditions, the tools designed to ensure an even playing field in college admissions were mastered to reproduce the disparities in society at large. What this tells us very simply is that the tool is broken. If I bought a spirit level to build a house and the house ended up crooked, I would buy a new level. I wouldn't invest a great deal of time figuring out exactly what was defective about the busted one. Maybe it used to work. Maybe it was fine for another project, but not leveling the tilt of my house.

In matters of race, however, the first assumption is that there is something wrong with black kids, their parents, and teachers. Certainly we invest great effort in trying to diagnose what's wrong with them, inventing new tests that are meant to hold teachers accountable and to measure progress "objectively" even as we ignore the objective data already there. These efforts inevitably fail, of course, because what's actually wrong is that society has done a number on them. Even such well-meaning interventions as Teach for America, in which kids from expensive schools with no teaching experience are dispatched across black, brown, Appalachian schools like so many miniature saviors, reek of colonialism. Those who stay I'm sure make a difference like any committed teacher. In reality, most are only passing through, like a tour in the Peace Corps. In reality, like diversity programs in general, it is at least as much of an investment in the liberal arts kids as in the students and schools they are allegedly serving. The underlying assumption, contrary to actual data, is what's wrong with ghetto schools is that they do not have enough white teachers.

Rather than running down this warren of broken things, why not simply abandon the tests, which do not work, and integrate the schools, which does? It's about belonging and class anxiety, of course, which happen to be proxies for race. The rise of testing and fetishization of a dozen universities in a country where there are thousands is in exact, inverse proportion to the shrinking of the American Dream and class mobility.

As long as black people are the ones who suffer, most Americans will accept that everything is working as it should. Lopsided houses and all. It is why people on the right and their liberal enablers—who are only in the business of their own houses, after all—devote so much time to test prep, strategizing ways to resegregate, moving to neighborhoods that happen to be whiter, or vying for places in magnet schools that use standardized tests as their primary admissions criteria. They have found an empirical instrument that guarantees the results they crave.

A country that actually wanted to make a test that truly measured merit would be able to do so, or at least invest more in the effort than America has. There would be grant money, contests, and billionaires tinkering on the weekends. If anyone wanted that. "The American education system has vestiges of engineered inequities," according to one of the many recent reports on school segregation sixty-five years after *Brown v. Board of Education*.[8] The sentence is so understated it's risible, until it is not: "and those inequities have created unequal opportunities for a huge chunk of black Americans. When we query the data using this framework, the answer is clear: We are going in reverse." People on the right indignantly dispute the claim that we are going backward. What's happening, they insist, torturing the data, is that things have stopped *improving*. As if staying where we are is all right.

Maybe in a noncolonial society the current test would be fine, maybe it could even account for a generation of disadvantage, but not a dozen generations who have been told the American Dream is not meant for them.

At present, 66 percent of African American children grow up in neighborhoods with significant poverty, as opposed to 6 percent of white children. Over 50 percent of them attend schools that are 90 to 100 percent black.[9] These are the same neighborhoods and schools that were engineered to be segregated by housing policy. School districts are, after all, still drawn around residential neighborhoods. If neighborhoods are segregated, schools will be. After the legal success of *Brown v. Board of Education* in the 1950s, the Federal Department of Education later adopted a policy making it illegal to use federal funds for transportation to integrate schools. It has remained on the books through Democratic and Republican regimes alike, as the number of black kids attending impoverished schools continues to grow.[10]

In New York City, after nine years of attending segregated, impoverished schools, students must take a test that measures mastery of subject matter to determine whether or not they may attend one of New York's elite high schools. After thirteen years of ghetto schooling, they sit for the SAT. The results are uneven, and test prep and expensive tutoring exacerbate this. One solution has been to offer free test prep to poor kids, as though a few months spent learning the tricks of the test can make up for going to school in the ghetto your government and fellow citizens spent eighty years building for you.

We play a shell game of pretending to "fix" the problem by teaching students to be better test takers. Of blaming black kids for being black, and punishing them for it.

If our real business is maintaining the status quo, while assuaging our conscience into thinking we are acting, then we are doing just fine. After all, it's only the black kids moving in reverse. If there was a similar problem in testing among Italian or Jewish or Irish students or any other group of Western European immigrants, we would conclude accurately that the test— and indeed the entire system of public education—wasn't doing what it was designed to do. America has always made special exceptions for black people this way.

Among the eight hundred colleges and universities in the United States that make reporting standardized test scores an optional part of admissions, researchers have found no statistical difference in student performance. Instead, "Almost all institutions in our study increased enrollment of underserved populations. . . . And, the policy transition occurred without any signs of academic slide: GPAs and graduation rates didn't suffer, and according to reports from the Deans many faculty were very pleased with the quality and character of the incoming classes."[11]

The universities that are test optional include major research institutions such as the University of Chicago and Wake Forest. The Admissions page on Wake Forest's website notes, "For the record, it's not that we think standardized tests are evil. We just think that the measure of your intelligence and potential requires a deeper dive. It's about life experience, aspiration, work ethic, engagement and all of what makes you who you are. That's why we believe so strongly in the interview process. Numbers rarely tell the whole story." Wake Forest is a private institution, less affected by legal attacks on affirmative action, but like all universities it cannot say that one of the aims of its admissions policy is to integrate the student body. Despite this, even at a place like the University of Chicago that has evidence of the efficacy of the new approach, the financial resources to do as it pleases, and a historical reputation for independence of thought, African American enrollment is a scant 9 percent. This places it not only behind national demographics but also behind many of its peers at the country's most selective colleges.[12]

In the case of Chicago, the dereliction of effort is even more striking because the school is located in the middle of the Southside of Chicago, one of the largest African American communities in the country. The school's relationship to this population is more vexed than town and gown, though, going back to the early twentieth-century invention of fields like sociology. It has often been one of active otherization. The student handbook actively discourages people from interacting with the surrounding area. To borrow briefly from personal experience of campuses like the University of Chicago that are located in the middle of historically African American neighborhoods, the pervasive mood-state is not simply the sense of superiority inculcated on the campuses of other schools that cater to the intellectual, moneyed, and hereditary elite. It is one of fear mirroring the larger police state, in which "safety" becomes a proxy for race. Certain streets are not to be crossed even during daylight hours. Certain faces elicit calls to the campus police. This incessantly reinforced fear of black people is a way of seeing I find I must consciously resist. Sometimes, I am ashamed to admit, I resist imperfectly. That is how the poison works. As long as you attend the right school, work for the right company, have enough money, and practice the right codes, including prejudices, then you may belong. Those who don't do not belong, and this is America: Who does not care to belong?

Public universities, the most vulnerable defendants in the four-decades-long attack on affirmative action, have seen part of their original purpose compromised. The point of land-grant institutions was to make high-quality education more accessible during the industrial revolution in a country where, historically, college was primarily for the few who could afford it, and the talent of those without money to pay rarely realized its full potential. In working so hard against integration the underlying reasoning is, of course, that black talent matters less than white talent. This warps the basic spirit of citizenship and mutual respect for young people, but also assumes that the schools— being public institutions—do not know their own business.

I know several exceptional people who did not test well but gained admission to Ivy League universities because the college counselors at their well-regarded high schools, or some other adult who cared what happened to them, was able to call an admissions officer, not to beg exception for the well-connected but, rightfully, to let the schools know here was somebody special whose talents weren't being properly reflected by the tests. Everyone should be so fortunate.

If we really believe in equal opportunity, why do we allow schools to remain in the half-state of desegregation they were in a generation ago, instead of pressing for greater integration or defending tools that are proven to work *counter* to our stated beliefs? "Because," my friend from the College Board argues, "the majority get the result they want." In the case of black kids it means a buffer class of the exceptional that liberals can point to as evidence of the good works of liberal institutions, while the system as a whole remains overwhelmingly segregated.

By embracing the pleasing surface of exceptionalism, our sense of complicity is ameliorated. We need the exceptional in order to convince ourselves that things are working and to heighten the feeling of accomplishment about how far we have come. In reality, we remain firmly inside a postcolonial frame. What the tests really measure isn't achievement but the exact tally of the effects of school segregation. What admissions officers are doing when they apply their own tools of "affirmative action" is simply correcting for some of the distortion in the field, often in ways that are not legible to laypeople, especially those with a retrograde agenda. This kind of affirmative action helps some of the exceptional to be accurately seen by tipping to correct the bias of a broken spirit level.

For many, even this small measure is too much. A recent lawsuit by Edward Blum, a conservative activist, accuses Harvard of unfairly discriminating against Asian Americans (who have the highest average SAT scores of any ethnic group). Mr. Blum has a history of bringing lawsuits that attack voting rights and affirmative action, most notably in Texas, where he made his living as a stockbroker before becoming a professional rabble-rouser for conservative goals. The angle this time is essentially that if you go strictly by the tests, you should admit more Asian kids and fewer blacks and Latinos.[13] When all the data were crunched, however, it turned out that the people actually getting the greatest benefit of subjective measures of merit when it came to admissions were white students, of whom 43 percent are "legacies," athletes, and the children of donors. According to the estimates of the plaintiffs' own witnesses, only 25 percent of them would have gotten in through the door facing the street if the only measures used were perfect grades and SAT scores.[14]

However, discrimination against this group or that is not the problem in this particular instance. It is balancing the interests of all its constituencies in a way that reflects Harvard's core values, two of which appear to be gathering interesting people from everywhere and loyalty within its existing community: a miniature of the country as a whole.

If everyone has more or less proportional access, it's hard to find fault with those goals, and it may actually be close to the most virtuous model. In real terms it means about six hundred people from the old school and twelve hundred new ones each year, across every demographic imaginable. It also happens to be near what the civil rights people originally proposed, which, of course, is why conservatives take issue with it. Of course they have also been programmed to think, like too many people, certain schools are Noah's ark and everyone else is meant to drown.

Top private universities in the United States now cost more than $240,000 for a four-year degree, with flagship public schools, such as the University of Michigan, not far behind. It is a figure that, give or take a couple of grand, represents a yearly cost that is the same as the median annual income in America. Big-brand education has become an increasingly luxurious commodity, and affirmative action, like the actual research that gets done beneath the preening, is one of the efforts that belongs to a different value system in which schools, whether public or private, are part of a national trust.

Ironically, the main aspect of its admissions policy that has come under fire is something Harvard calls *character*, an intangible whose meaning we may well have forgotten. Let's imagine for a moment it is what it implies, a rubric under which to consider the whole person or simply a way to weed out persons of low, troublesome virtue. Without knowing the first thing about how the good people of Cambridge sort themselves from others, it seems self-evident that no one wants to be in a place filled with thousands of scheming Iagos. Distinctions of character are lost, of course, on the ghoulish neo-Confederate machinery that has been singularly focused on overturning the gains of the civil rights movement, trafficking as it does in amorality, sanctimony, and mischievous faith. After all, part of what universities are meant to do is not simply give golden tickets to high-status jobs but serve as hubs where the best minds and spirits are nurtured and trained to keep inventing and dreaming even in ways that may be hard to measure.

Not everyone aims to knock the cover off the ball—from here to the continent's divide. There are millions of intelligent people whose grand dream is a life of quiet decency and well-being, nothing more extravagant than the shelter of family, work, and community. This used to be called the American Dream, and it was once assumed to be universally available, or at least not delusional. But if education is still the main line of national mobility, the current course of segregation and underinvestment in the public commons is a slow road to a bad place that only those who actively seek to inflict suffering would create.

There are approximately 3.7 million high school graduates per year, of whom 545,000 are black. There are 173,000 places in the entering class across the fifty best-regarded universities in the country. If all of them had an enrollment that was 13.4 percent African American, slightly more than 23,000 black kids would receive seats, 26,000 if we add the top fifty liberal arts colleges.[15] What happens to all the others?

If we confine our goal to getting 30 percent (the national average) of black kids into college, we need to find places for 160,000 kids each year. If we look at all the seats in the freshman class across the four hundred most selective colleges, one would have to admit black kids at the rate of 12 percent universally. But one also finds that the number of kids, across all ethnic groups, living in poverty is alone half the total capacity of the system.[16] At the current rate, the problem will never be fixed.

There are rough numbers, of course, but even as a thought experiment it should be clear there is a lot more to worry about than the 236 black kids and 412 Asian American kids (good for all of them) who got themselves into Harvard this year. Yet liberals will look at the numbers, 12 percent of Harvard's class, and see a triumph. These same numbers, like anything we do to advance equality, will be seen as cause for alarm among conservatives, including the court justices who have throttled affirmative action in education to its current levels. Testing is the least part of the problem.

When we are honest, it is clear how much closer we are to the beginning than the end of what might fairly be called America's Cold Civil War, a state of détente in which the forces of the Civil War continue to dictate American politics. The South and its sympathizers press in every way to limit democracy and opportunity to as few as possible and to preserve special privileges for whites. Northerners hate the idea of such oppression but are so deeply enmeshed that they lack the will and clarity to eradicate it. Everyone suffers, of course, but that's a price millions are willing to ignore so long as pain traces the axis of race and people of color hurt twice as much.

8

THE MAINSTREAMING OF BLACK MUSIC

For there they that carried us away captive required of us a song; and they that wasted us required of us mirth, saying, Sing us one of the songs of Zion.

—Psalms 137:3

I was mesmerized the first time I heard Public Enemy. It was the summer after my sophomore year of high school, and a kid I'll call Ismael, who had moved from New York, played the group's first album, *Yo! Bum Rush the Show*, one day when we were gathered in the park. Sure, I'd heard the ubiquitous party anthem "Rapper's Delight," which we used to roller skate to, but this was altogether different, sonically and politically. The main line of black music in America is profoundly encoded, and the message on the grapevine is, usually, one way or another I intend to be free.

Chuck D, the front man, made no attempt to hide it. Instead of doo-wop girls harmonizing in the background there was a DJ called Terminator X and a phalanx of brothers, who looked still upset about Vietnam, in military fatigues, doing a step routine while brandishing mock Uzis. At least I *think* they were only props. Flava Flav played the clown to leaven the message, but the overall attitude harkened back to Malcolm X and an age of political indignation that had long faded away. It was less than twenty-five years after Malcolm had been killed, but that was longer than I had been alive, and it seemed to me then much further away.

Along with rappers like KRS-One, De La Soul, the Jungle Brothers, and A Tribe Called Quest (most of them part of a loose collective known as Zulu Nation), Public Enemy represented a musical reclamation of Afrocentrism and Black Power. It was also infused with the sound of New York's downtown punk scene, another subculture of sonic rebellion, the cocaine epidemic, and the conservative "War on Drugs," which mostly meant locking black people in prison by the hundreds of thousands. Public Enemy's music was literally about jailbreak and figuratively about all the concentric prisons of the carceral state. It was provocative and, if you happened to see anything wrong with the national state of affairs, was empowering. If you did not, it was dangerous. In the layering of musical influences and its outspokenness it seemed to speak to the age I was living in— the most celebrated black people of the time, Michael Jackson and Michael Jordan, were judiciously nonpolitical—better than anything else. Black music has always been ahead of other art forms in America.

The other instances I remember being arrested in the same way were the first time I heard Jimi Hendrix, Bob Marley, John

Coltrane, Pink Floyd, Paul Simon, and Miles in his weird phase. At the time I thought I was simply discovering new music from the cool kids, usually with even cooler older siblings. In retrospect, as my experience of art began to reshape my consciousness, I realized that I was being formed. They were complete experiences of a kind I had only encountered before while reading: visceral, intellectual, creative, psychological. Reflections of the way I already saw that reaffirmed who I was, but also new ways of seeing and new patterns to measure the world against as I was born again for the first time, unto myself and not simply my family's or society's dutiful child.

The music I knew before—Motown, Parliament, Kool & the Gang, Stevie Wonder—important as it was to me, was my parents' music. This new music was validating my own interior life but also increasing it with more sophistication than I possessed at the time, and deep beneath it all, as I learned what it was to truly listen, it was teaching me instruments and structures to invent my own song. There were other things I would come to love in the future, or was taught to love, but these were naive reactions to originality that would ever after influence the way I listened and heard.

Discovering black music, its spirituals, its rebellions, its beauty, its uniquely New World anguish and genius, was also a process of connecting to black culture. There's a reason Frederick Douglass, in his first autobiography, says that to understand slavery you had to hear the song of slaves on holiday, when "they would make the dense old woods, for miles around, reverberate with their wild songs, revealing at once the highest joy and the deepest sadness."[1] Similarly, Du Bois's masterwork, *The Souls of Black Folk*, written a generation after Emancipation, when it had already become clear the country had no intention of giving black people anything remotely resembling a square deal, employs a constant refrain of music when there were no more slaves but the woods still reverberated. A blues song.

I still remember the furtive smile my grandfather gave me when I was first discovering this canon and he discovered what I was listening to. "You like that stuff?" he asked, with a bemused expression. I nodded. "When I was a young man, we all were trying to get away from all that." For me, for reasons I was still coming to understand, it seemed of burning importance to stay connected.

It would take seven years before I was mesmerized by anything in the same way as my first encounter with Public Enemy. It was a summer afternoon in New Orleans, and my friend Kevin came by my apartment on Magazine Street in his seagreen Honda Accord. We were going to an event in Congo Square, the old African meeting place, where blacks used to gather on Sundays to trade goods, make music, and dance and, like the Mississippi River itself, one of the places in that town where one still felt a rip in the seam of the world.

When I got in the car, Kevin grinned sheepishly and took out a CD, announcing he had something I just had to hear. Kevin, unfailingly courteous, mild-mannered, an achiever, practiced the politics of southern black respectability, which made it all the more disquieting when he popped *Ready to Die* by Notorious B.I.G. into the stereo and turned up the volume. It was the most vulgar thing I had ever heard. It was also unstintingly violent. Although groups like NWA also rapped about violence, that was protest. This was nihilism distilled. Existential desensitization as weapon and shield. Or so it seemed to me then. Kevin and I debated the rest of that afternoon whether it was, in fact, as people in those days were arguing, bad for black America.

Decades later, listening to the album through a pair of high-fidelity speakers built to reveal every nuance in the source material, I'm struck by something altogether different. Today—when the rap industry generates $10 billion in yearly revenue, and the wealthiest rapper (Biggie's old running partner), Jay Z, is himself a billionaire—Biggie, who told of middle-market brand aspirations and "just tryin' to make some money so I can feed my daughter," sounds innocent.

Christopher Wallace, Notorious B.I.G.'s given name, was communicating the individual and shared lifeworld of his experience running drugs and trying to raise a family in the Brooklyn ghetto during the height of the crack plague. His listeners heard it as a metaphor for the black struggle at the turn of the twenty-first century.

In the years since Biggie's old neighborhood has been gentrified, hip-hop has been embraced by a mainstream seeking the same authenticity generations of white Americans have long sought in black music. For most it represents their only exposure to black life. Because of this, many observers, including rappers like Nas and Azalia Banks who remain close to the form's more political roots, have accused those who produce the most popular strands of hip-hop (which tend to traffic in representations of drug life and have become the dominant music form in contemporary America) of being a minstrel show, giving whites the stereotypes of black life they long to see and believe.

The cultural product of an artist does not necessarily belong to the artist's racial group, but hip-hop has long prided itself on being black music, a unique and uniquely authentic representation of African American life. When the mainstream listens to it, it is often with the sense of absorbing a forbidden cultural experience, a form of crossing the tracks to the other side of town, but also bridging racial divides. Once you can appreciate someone's culture, it becomes much harder to dehumanize them. At least that is the theory.

What happens when one performs the cliché for an outside audience for profit? What is the effect of the feedback loop of cultural output and market acceptance? The tension between authenticity and mass media, in which cultural output is increasingly determined by market pressure, has been a central facet of bourgeois American culture. Economic incentives are now crowd-sourced, for better and worse, fundamentally changing what artists make, or at least the art the public patronizes, instead of art shaping how people see, read, hear, and understand the world.

In hip-hop, commercialization has pushed art toward a celebration of materialism that accords with mainstream American values, in which the wildly successful businessman is a cultural hero and the best artist is a canny, Warholian capitalist. When we celebrate hip-hop for uniting us across the divide of race, or as the heir to the huge canon of black music, what we critique or celebrate depends on what version of rap music we subscribe to and what has informed the listening experience. Surrounding it all is the ever-present question of performance and appropriation. What level of access to black culture can nonblacks have? Who "owns" the music, yes, but what is the role of race in creation and interpretation? What are you making, for whom and why?

Of the best-selling rap artists in the genre's history, three are white, and their works say as much about the form as anything, the ways it is understood by the mainstream, and the role of race in our deep interior lives and public self-presentation.

The Beastie Boys were the first nonblack group to achieve widespread success and legitimacy in rap. Raised by middle-class professionals in Brooklyn, they began as a punk band, and their work combines these underground forms. Russell Simmons and Rick Rubin, the founders, one black and the other white and Jewish, of the seminal label DefJam, saw in them the potential to "cross a lot of boundaries that a lot of other rap groups couldn't."[2]

As the partnership of Simmons and Rubin suggests, many of the people behind the music commonly crossed these lines in their lives, but the wider culture remained largely segregated. Hip-hop is a form of musical L.H.O.O.Q., named for one of the artworks of Marcel Duchamp, in which the artist transforms ready-made, ordinary objects into something radical and new. What the hip-hop artists were finding was samples not only from other musicians but also from film, television, brand marketing, popular culture, and, most crucially, all of music. It was the sound, whatever else one thinks about it, of complex experience channeled through complex young people.

The Beastie Boys' debut album, *Licensed to Ill*, is the work of connoisseurs and rebels, but also teenage cutups in the John Hughes (Ferris Bueller) mold. They are less pure rappers than musical experimentalists, and one has the sense that as artists they would have discovered whatever was most interesting and daring in the world around them. In 1980s New York, that was punk and rap. The album in turn brought into the tent a number of white listeners who otherwise might not have paid attention to rap music, which was the design that Rubin and Simmons, shrewdly or cynically, intended. It was cultural boundary cross-ing as a political and creative statement from a group whose members were born in the years immediately after the Civil Rights Act, but also a savvy business move.

The history of black music, of course, most notably rock-and-roll, is rife with stories of white artists who appropriated or stole outright material from black creators or who enjoyed a success with the mainstream unattainable by their black peers. It was a lesson rap has always been anxious to avoid but also, like the DefJam team (whose other senior member was Lyor Cohen, who would later become global boss at Sony Music), to use in cat-and-mouse games of titillation. Not everyone was in equal control.

Robert Van Winkle personified those fears when his single "Ice Ice Baby" became the first rap song to top the charts. His act bore the unmistakable influence of the black rapper MC Ham-mer, himself viewed as a commercial lightweight to most fans of the genre. It was rap as pure mainstream entertainment, music to dance to, not think about. As a musician, in a form that prized originality, there was little to distinguish him. Still, he reached a level of success unavailable to black rappers at the time. In many ways it was a novelty act. The gimmick, of course, was watching a white performer mimic his black coun-terparts. But unlike even a performer such as Elvis (who turned on people like Bob Dylan and was convinced unto himself his was a fated assignation with blackness), it was clear Vanilla Ice was just passing through. Whatever Van Winkle's authorial in-tentions, the mainstream embraced him as it never had a black hip-hop act, in what was still derided as not being music or, as the euphemism then went, was merely "urban."

In the video for "Ice Ice Baby" it is readily apparent that all involved understand they are performing race, and there is something deeply unsettling about the performance. The opening montage—spray cans writing the word *Ice* in graffiti on a brick wall—invokes early movies about the genre, like *Beat Street* and the dance-oriented *Breakin'*, which were widely respected by fans. However, the palette, neon pink and green, has more in common with groups like New Kids on the Block, signaling a remove from the gritty context usually associated with the form. The camera then lingers on a mural of legendary jazz musician Louis Armstrong, mouth to trumpet, cheeks distended, eyes wide, before cutting to a group of black girls on the street. Three early tropes of the form in quick succession to establish its bona fides. It is only after waving these talismans that Van Winkle's square-jawed face appears, almost apologetic (to his credit the man looks self-aware enough to be ashamed), before launching into an energetic dance routine, surrounded by an all-black chorus worthy of Oedipus, wearing the full red, black, and green investiture of Afrocentrism to lend still more symbolic weight to the tragedy about to unfold.

Rap was not yet the most popular music in America, as it would become, but Vanilla Ice quickly become the most famous rapper, his whiteness and the slightness of the music giving license to other white people to let themselves enjoy instead of castigate it, which is exactly what was happening on the stage of national politics, as its critics sought to censor or otherwise control it. Rap—in its musical miscegenation, its violence, its sexual swagger—was threatening. Vanilla Ice was entertainment, and as many after him would learn, there is more money to be had, and friends to be made, in making people dance than in cultural critiques.

Marshall Mathers was born in St. Joseph, Missouri, and moved to Detroit as a boy, coming of age in that city's music scene, where as an outsider in an outsider genre he first proved himself as a battle rapper—the hip-hop equivalent of a showdown with the devil at the crossroads—a rapper's rapper.

He was also bankable. After partnering with the producer Andre Young, who had risen to fame under the stage name Dr. Dre, Marshall's first studio album, *The Slim Shady LP*, sold more than ten million copies and won that year's Grammy for best rap album. Many whites saw in him proof that white people could succeed, indeed excel, in the form. But Mathers was more than the latest white Prometheus going to the other side of town to bring back blues. In his anger at the lot he was born to, his challenge of authority, his fluency in the culture, which included a deft knowledge of where offense lay, including the offense of cultural appropriation or claims of being the Great White Hope some of his fans saw in him, there was naturalness, authenticity, irreverence as a hard-won originality.

He raps about a form of struggle—"I can't get by with my nine to five"—usually confined, among white musicians, to country music. Unlike most country musicians, he wasn't glorifying or masking but damning his struggle, the kind of struggle usually said to be reserved for black people. His lyrics are filled with shame and rage and desperation, the lowest lows of

American life, and defiance to survive it. Whiteness is about the performance of control. His was a music of being out of control, overwhelmed by circumstances, outcast, and desperate for the shelter of blackness.

White people have always looked to black music for the same reason black people have: a salvation otherwise unavailable in secular American materialism. Mathers was making no attempt to hide how plaintively deep that need went, admitting for anyone who cared to hear that a career in whiteness wasn't really working for him, and not what he envisioned for his future.

In common with many of his contemporaries, Mathers grew up poor, without benefit of formal training, perhaps even without a basic musical education, attending the kinds of schools made for poor people, but nevertheless managing to master the greatest instrument there is: the human voice.

I'm not certain what white people see when they look at him, the rare white person capable or willing to meet black culture on its own terms without having to do the work themselves, a way to enjoy black culture without interrupting their long holiday apart, or fuel for the fantasy that anything black can be stolen.

Black people judged him on the merits. As a rapper he was among the best, a student of the form itself, capable of communicating his own pain, beneath it a more essential knowledge about depths of experience beyond the reach of the world. He also knew what it was to be an outsider and work twice as hard, not merely for success and toleration but also for belonging. He was one of the few whites in music who wasn't looking for inspiration to carry back into the white world, but willing to pay the price for a seat at the table, where the stakes are your very life, and one of the few whites in any walk of American life to acknowledge integration as a two-way street.

Black music is the sound of liberation, even in the extremes of privation, despair, whatever form of tribulation—the highest self. American music itself is, regardless of who is performing, deeply black. Blacker than most whites can admit, just as they cannot admit, or genuinely do not know, what a black place—at once the highest joy and the deepest sadness—America has always been. Someday we shall all be free.

9

PASTIME

True heroism is remarkably sober, very undramatic. It is
not the urge to surpass all others at whatever cost, but
the urge to serve others at whatever cost.

—Arthur Ashe, *On Tennis*

The game of lacrosse was invented in Algonquin country by
the first people of that nation, in what would come to be
called the St. Lawrence River Valley. It was originally a martial
art, thought to train young men to be warriors, but played as
well for relaxation and, it is said, religious reasons, not unlike
sport and war everywhere.

The first European accounts of the game date to 1630,
when French missionaries ventured into the area. The rules of
the modern contest began to coalesce in the middle of the nineteenth century, as it grew to become Canada's national sport.
Queen Victoria, while viewing an exhibition in London in 1876,
is said to have remarked, "The game is very pretty to watch."[1] It

is a sentiment usually reserved for soccer, "the beautiful game," which it resembles if you imagine a soccer match played by two teams colliding into each other while running, cradling, passing, and shooting an object the size of a tennis ball but twice as heavy, with netted sticks the size of a hand.

According to most knowledgeable students of lacrosse, Jim Brown played and dominated this game more beautifully than anyone else who has ever walked onto the field. "I coached this game for 46 years," Roy Simmons, who long led perennial powerhouse Syracuse, recalled when Brown was inducted into the Lacrosse Hall of Fame, "and Jim Brown was the greatest lacrosse player I ever saw."

Fewer than thirty seconds have survived of his years on the field. An 8-millimeter film clip, oxidized with time, captures Brown as he faces off against an opponent at midfield, explodes through traffic, cradling his stick with one hand, breaking free, joyful as a child from the schoolhouse door, before converting to a two-handed grip as he feints through a scrum for thirty yards, a man now in full exultation, until the camera pans to him jogging casually back upfield. By the time the defenders realize he has scored, Brown is already preparing for the next play, his move on goal faster than his opponents or the shutter can see.[2]

"I could fully express myself in lacrosse," Brown recalled in 1984, after retiring from sports, still remembering its joys vividly nearly thirty years after his last competitive match. "I could run 200 yards at a stretch, I could duck between players. I felt free to make plays that suited me best. It wasn't like football then and basketball today, where coaches tell you what foot to put down."[3]

Brown was born in 1936 in the Sea Islands of Georgia, once famous for its cotton, and moved to Long Island as a boy, where he first learned to play lacrosse. For a black man born two generations after slavery, it was a feeling of freedom rare to find in any public sphere in America.

He had an equally impressive career in the NFL, of course, where he earned his greatest fame. He led the game in rushing yards for eight of the nine seasons he played, earning the title Most Valuable Player in the league three of those years. When he retired, at the age of thirty, he had rushed more yards than anyone in the history of the NFL, and even today, when the length of the season is a third longer, he remains eleventh on the all-time list.

Brown was so good that he began to grow bored and parlayed his fame on the field to an acting career. At the start of the 1966 football season, he was on location in London filming the movie *The Dirty Dozen* when production delays threatened to make him miss the start of training camp. As the NFL preseason grew ever nearer, Art Modell, owner of the Cleveland Browns, issued a statement publicly chastising Brown, saying in part:

> No veteran Browns player has been granted or will be given permission to report late to our training camp . . . —and this includes Jim Brown. Should Jim fail to report to [camp] at check-in time deadline . . . I will have no alternative [but] to suspend him without pay. I recognize the complex problems of the motion picture business, having spent several years in the industry. However, in all fairness to everyone connected with the Browns—the coaching staff, the players and most

important of all, our many faithful fans—I feel compelled to say that I will have to take such action should Jim be absent on July 17.

Brown responded to this public rebuke in a private letter to Modell:

> I am writing to inform you that in the next few days I will be announcing my retirement from football. This decision is final and is made only because of the future that I desire for myself, my family and, if not to sound corny, my race. I am very sorry that I did not have the information to give you at some earlier date, for one of my great concerns was to try in every way to work things out so that I could play an additional year.
>
> I was very sorry to see you make the statements that you did, because it was not a victory for you or I but for the newspaper men. Fortunately, I seem to have a little more faith in you than you have in me. I honestly like you and will be willing to help you in any way I can, but I feel you must realize that both of us are men and that my manhood is just as important to me as yours is to you.[4]

Days later, in an interview with *Sports Illustrated*, he made his decision public: "I could have played longer. I wanted to play this year, but it was impossible. We're running behind schedule shooting here, for one thing. I want more mental stimulation than I would have playing football. I want to have a hand in the struggle that is taking place in our country."[5]

Months earlier, Malcolm X had been assassinated. Two years earlier, the civil rights leader Medgar Evers was brutally slain by a member of a Mississippi group formed to resist school integration. In the same year, Lyndon Johnson had overcome significant congressional resistance to pass the Civil Rights Act of 1964, based on the Civil Rights Act of 1875.

As an athlete and actor, Brown commanded a degree of visibility and public respect unavailable to black people in most realms of society. He understood himself as a role model and, like other black athletes before him, a spokesman.

Before it got wise on steroids and data, baseball, the old national pastime, was in the business of selling the myth of American wholesomeness: pastoral virginity, possibility, and fair play, no matter that the game was segregated and many of the best players in the country were forbidden to compete. Football, America's game, has always been unapologetically about gladiators in the imperial circus. A blood sport in whose Colosseum defeat belongs to the vanquished and victory, as in Rome, to the sponsor, who, as one might expect, desires obeisance.

Fifty years after Brown refused to bend the knee to Modell, quarterback Colin Kaepernick knelt when he wasn't supposed to, during the recital of the national anthem, an act of protest meant to add visibility to the struggle for accountability in the epidemic of police brutality. As a new generation of Americans became newly aware of the previously undertold number of executions of black men at the hands of police across the country, the same problem that inspired the Panthers had brought people of Kaepernick's generation to political awareness.

Young people across the country were using camera phones to do the same thing the Panthers had done in Oakland, stop as citizens in the proverbial dark to bear witness. Just as the real problem of police violence, and the social forces that consciously or not sanction it, was an old one, so the perceived "problem" of Kaepernick, a black man protesting white social violence in 2016, led to the same fate that befell Jim Brown in 1966 for asserting his agency.

Sport in America has always been a proxy for other national narratives, as a realm of perceived freedom, one of the few where everyone is said to compete in an arena of objectively fair rules. In a nation eternally riven by race it is also a natural analogy for the state of the race game: a measure of the degree of fairness accorded athletes of different social identity, a mirror for group pride or ascendancy, a proxy for race war, and a public forum to extol the powers of the body. If the body is threatening, like Roman gladiators, who were often slaves from a defeated army but always from the lowest social classes, subdue it again symbolically for public consumption to demonstrate the power of the sponsor and affirm for the audience its own superior social status. A barbarian or slave life is a Roman's sport and entertainment.

As a gladiator might win either death or freedom, our narrative of sport also serves, we are told, as a metaphor of transcendence and healing. In this mode the lone black athlete clears the hurdles of exclusion that whiteness erects—Jackie Robinson stoically tolerating being called names for six months of the year, the Williams sisters conquering the record books despite years of crowd hostility and unequal sponsorship money, or Stanford-educated Tiger Woods, back when he was Cablinasian (a portmanteau to signify uniqueness and not-really-blackness), instead of black and Filipino. Or, like Muhammad

Ali, the baddest motherfucker around. Ali died with far less than he would have had he acted good and grateful or like just one of the boys.

Ali was also denied the right to compete for three years after refusing to join the war against Vietnam. Being the best after that didn't always mean the most titles but also walking the tightrope between personal interests and the sacrifices of being a spokesman. Jordan (called Yahweh in his inner circle) kept his mouth shut, modeling the sportsman as corporate not public citizen, and became a multibillionaire. In America even God has His price.

When Kaepernick, one of only a handful of black quarterbacks in the NFL's history, refused to stand for the national anthem, vast portions of America were upset or enthralled, depending on prior political views. This protest led ultimately to the end of Kaepernick's career in football; Donald Trump called for him to be expelled from the league. This time it wasn't just between a player and an owner, but a contest of manhood with the president of the United States. A gladiator refusing to bow to the emperor and so affirm the lies of greatness that the shriveled race state still wishes to believe.

In a deposition after he was blacklisted, Kaepernick sued the NFL for collusion. It soon came to light, according to Dallas Cowboys owner Jerry Jones, that Donald Trump told him the NFL protests were "a very winning, strong issue for me. Tell everybody, you can't win this one. This one lifts me."[6] He meant more NFL fans were on his side than on Kaepernick's.

Trump has a long history of demonizing black people, beginning in the late 1980s, when he bought newspaper ads to call for the death penalty for a group of black kids who had been charged with the rape of a white woman. The men were later exonerated after serving years in prison for a crime they did not commit. By that point Donald Trump had moved on to birtherism, questioning whether the nation's first black president had indeed been born in the United States. When that faded away, he seized on Kaepernick, questioning, as he did with Obama, his right to belong in America. He would do the same thing later with four women of color who were members of Congress, then again with civil rights hero Jim Clyburn. When Clyburn proved too wily to take the bait, Trump went after his old foil from the eighties, Al Sharpton. The man was stuck on repeat, but so were the media that always rewarded him (with more ego supply), and so was the country.

After calling for the firing of any player who protested during the national anthem, the emperor saw that it tested well with his focus group and escalated his rhetoric: "Maybe they shouldn't be in the country."[7] Who needed click-bait anymore? NFL attendance and viewership fell as Nero's rhetoric intensified.

Seventy percent of current NFL players are black.[8] In the domestic market, 83 percent of fans are white, some 95.5 million people.[9] African Americans account for another 15 percent of the league's fans, or 17.25 million people. If the fans, like the country as a whole, are evenly divided between conservatives and liberals, the conservative fan base is approximately 31 million people more than the total of its African American fans, whatever their political ideology. These are rough numbers—they aren't weighted to consider the fact that the Republican Party is 86 percent white, meaning that white NFL fans are more likely to be Republican and that appealing to racial resentment has long been a core of the Republican strategy—but one gets an idea of how many people Trump could incite against Kaepernick, or for that matter the owners.[10] The little emperor was having the time of his life.

The average NFL player is 6 feet, 3 inches tall and weighs 225 pounds. The fastest clocks in at 4.22 seconds over a forty-yard dash. The strongest can bench-press 250 pounds forty-nine times. The players earn a minimum salary of $480,000 and a league average of $2.7 million per year (≈$1.2 million after taxes and agents' commissions, which the league caps at 3 percent). The highest paid, Russell Wilson, earns an annual salary of $35 million.

The average team is worth $2.9 billion, and the owners hail from some of the wealthiest families in the country. The richest, technology tycoon Steve Ballmer, is worth $55 billion. The owner with the thinnest balance sheet, and the only one who is not a billionaire, has assets of $500 million.[11]

Trump, famously insecure about his place in the blue-chip aristocracy, equally insecure about his manhood, and rebuffed by the league when he tried to buy an NFL team, had the whole game by the balls. In the wake of the president's bullying, no team owner—which includes only two people of color, both Asian Americans—would hire Kaepernick.

The owners blinked. The quarterback didn't. Who do you want on your team?

Sport is—besides a proxy for war, self, and power—ultimately a narrative of nationhood.

Modern sports were central to life and identity in the British Empire, which bequeathed this legacy to no country more than the United States. As immigrants from Europe crossed the Atlantic, they were soon inculcated in the culture of sport as a way of Americanizing them. Blacks were excluded from most major competitions until shortly after World War II, when, owing to a variety of pressures, baseball was famously integrated by Jackie Robinson.

A year earlier the NFL was also integrated, albeit with less fanfare. The game was not as popular as it is today, when it has supplanted baseball as the national pastime and grown into the richest sports league in the country, with $14 billion in annual revenue. There have been only thirty-seven black quarterbacks, the most visible position in the game, across all thirty-two teams in one hundred years.

The same discrimination that once swore colored men were not evolutionarily fit enough to challenge whites would morph through the subconscious, after evidence disproved this first slander, into its opposite, the equally racist assertion that African American athletes are genetically superior and owe their success to the conditions of slavery. Anything to avoid the truth that we are all equally endowed. The rest is a question of what you do with it, which depends on opportunity. "Well, they've got everything; if [blacks] take over coaching like everybody wants them to, there's not going to be anything left for white people," the former CBS commentator Jimmy "The Greek" Snyder said, apropos of absolutely nothing, in a 1988 interview, after being asked about the significance of Martin Luther King Day. "The black is a better athlete to begin with, because he's been bred to be that way. Because of his high thighs and big thighs that go up

into his back. And they can jump higher and run faster because
of their bigger thighs, you see."[12]

There are two appeals to neo-Confederate attitudes in Snyder's statement. The first is that if blacks are allowed into the
management of the sport, they will displace whites. Management should be a white preserve. The second, "because he's bred
to be that way," calls on the history of slavery to reduce the athlete to an animal that has been bred, stripping the individual of
personal agency in his own success, but also identifying with
one who owns slaves and assuming that others will as well. It
was the white slaver who turned the savage, weak African into a
gridiron demigod.

Snyder said this on television, without self-consciousness,
comfortable that his 1980s audience would see as he saw, as Art
Modell saw in 1966. It's about manhood. White masculinity
versus black masculinity (leaving aside the homoerotic element
of the comment), white capital versus the black body it is being deployed to subjugate. Entertainment is never simply fun
and games, but a visceral identification for audience and critical
commentator alike, a desire to see the self and assert one's own
narrative onto a field, even beyond, perhaps especially beyond
one's own ability. When the bodies are black, watching and pre-
senting, which was Snyder's job, are about majority control of
the narrative. Of course he thought his audience would agree
with him. If it sounds unconscionably perverse, it is, at least until you recall you are talking about the kind of men who would
sell their own children.

After the importation of slaves was abolished, there were in
fact, as E. Franklin Frazier notes with academic understatement
in *The Negro Family in the United States*, "masters who, without

any regard for the preferences of their slaves, mated their human chattel as they did their stock."[13] The goal was the increase of supply available for labor or for sale.

There is no evidence that people were being bred for anything in particular, except their blackness. Traits of the type Snyder asserted occur in genetic isolation, and African Americans are the most genetically mixed people in the world. It also requires millennia to affect a human gene pool. The claim is impossible. I bother to refute it only because racists still continue to peddle false scientific claims, a nexus of the American obsession with both technology and race.

More simply, it's wrong all around. But in evoking such history one is making another kind of claim, which is meant in the white mind to redound to white credit: the horrors of history, reshaped into a perverse new claim of superiority and power of control. The prowess of the individual does not belong to the individual; it is a trait of the breed, and white people bred them. It rises from and activates in turn the strata of the subconscious where whiteness is inscribed, but also terror.

In 1988, when Snyder made his comment, Nelson Mandela was still in prison in South Africa.

It is difficult for many to accept that no genetic cluster or culture is superior or inferior to any other. Culture is a function of the human. But surely there is something special about my group, besides my own attachment to it. Cultures aren't static, but in constant shift. The current flux, for those used to colonial power, is greater than all of history before it, a real threat, as unnerving as civil rights. A threat that can be wielded by ethnonationalists to divide and inflame and seize control for their own purposes. But really the oldest ancient projection, and funniest joke ever made in Rome. Barbarians at the gate.

In 2004 comedian Chris Rock would feel comfortable enough to make a joke about such subterranean veins of thought for a mixed audience: "During slavery, they used to take the biggest, strongest slaves and breed them, and try their best to make big, strong super slaves—and there's evidence of that today, like the NFL for instance. NFL stands for Nigger Fuckin' Large. They bred the slaves, and this is why black people dominate every physical activity in the United States of America, OK? We're only 10 percent of the population, [but] we're 90 percent of the Final Four."[14]

It is anxiety over history you are uncomfortable with, and the body you can no longer control. What happens after the slaves have revolted? No one wants a joke explained to them, but the reason this one works is because it speaks the taboo aloud: we regard the black body differently, and we fear a future when it is fully master of itself.

Quantitatively, Kaepernick, as the NFL's apologists never tired of saying in their search for a whitewash of plausible deniability, was not the best quarterback in the league the year he was cut. Nor was he the worst. Not by a long shot. Qualitatively, he had led his team to a Super Bowl four years earlier and the NFC Championship the year after that. He had held the game in his hands for a season, which, empirically, by the law of sport makes him a champion ever after. When the owners and networks canceled him, he was twenty-eight years old and still very much in his prime, but a disposable sacrifice to the narrative of whiteness. "In the NFL they got a bunch of old white men owning teams and they got that slave mentality," NBA star LeBron James remarked in a 2018 interview, weighing in, among other issues, on Kaepernick's ban from football. "And it's like, 'This is my team. You do what the fuck I tell y'all to do. Or we get rid of y'all.'"[15]

James went on to voice the widely held conception of players' disposability, the "slave mentality" that holds sway in those who, by dint of buying ownership in a brand, believe they in fact own men. Certainly that seems to be the perception among athletes, who also point to the NFL's years-long conspiracy to suppress evidence of the damage the game inflicts on players, who play on average a little more than three years, often suffering debilitating injury and astronomical rates of chronic traumatic encephalopathy (CTE). They are simply bodies that may be disposed of after they have served their purpose: "The . . . NBA is what we believe [a player] can be. . . . In the NFL, it's like what can you do for me this Sunday, or this Monday or this Thursday. And if you ain't it, we moving on."[16]

NFL players command a great deal less social power than athletes in the NBA, the league wherein black players have the most power. Even there pay is kept artificially low, and the fifty-eight franchise owners earn the same as the five hundred players in the league. Players are also powerless to get rid of a noxious owner, like the Knicks' Jim Dolan. And although an increasing number of players are assuming positions in team and league management, only one, Michael Jordan, has become wealthy enough to buy a team. The owners in all leagues will claim, of course, they are due greater proceeds because of their capital at risk.

But money is cheaper than talent, and owners are at least as replaceable as players. NFL players—fast as sprinters, strong as weight lifters, studious as chess masters, with a work ethic few

understand—are high among the ranks of the greatest athletes
in the world. Certainly there is no game on Earth, save boxing, that exacts as great a toll on body, mind, and spirit. Despite
this, we are led to believe their bodies are of lesser value to sport
than the owners' money or the marketing money captured by
the league as a whole.

Aside from the narrative of capitalism, Kaepernick's case
tells on the black body that is also "biracial." Historically, the
"mixed" body has been alternately a buffer between black and
white, an exoticized desire object, and also, among those who
subscribe to purist racial thinking, seditious by virtue of existing. In addition to that terror, and the division of families
common to all enslaved African American history, there is yet
another element of illegitimacy, one that the Virginia House of
Burgesses took special pains to inscribe in order to eradicate any
lingering confusion, in law or society, from the era before the
slave codes of 1705. The biracial body was not free, nor, by the
time the slave codes were written in the revolutionary South,
was it ever to be freed.

At the time of Emancipation one million of the four million former bondspeople in America were of mixed European
and African ancestry. The body as witness to a crime. The body
as witness to the advanced pathology whereby you don't only
claim ownership of an "other"; you claim ownership of your kin
as well. The body as refutation of the absurdist myth that there
is any difference between white bodies and other bodies. The
assertion that the "mixed" body is inherently tragic. The body
as site of all pain. But ultimately, to the extent those one million

were related to those who claimed to own them, the body as proof and witness to a degeneracy absolute. One of the arguments at the Revolution for allowing the South into the Union was that it was the only way to save not blacks from whites but whites from themselves.

Frederick Douglass wondered all his life whether his owner was his father. If not, which man in that family had sired him. The custom followed by some slave owners, like Thomas Jefferson, was to make special exception for their children, setting them up in trade or bequeathing them enough to purchase an education. That might sound commendable, but only if your frame of reference is already the perversion of all things human. The delta between the two is the subject at hand.

The biracial body also harbors, however uncomfortably, the literal possibility of union and reconciliation. It is a reconciliation white people historically reject (one drop) but in contemporary times also wish to apply to the increasing number of Americans of multiple "racial" heritages to create a post-slavery buffer between themselves and the frightening original. In return for slightly fairer treatment by the majority, the light-complected body in colonial societies was supposed to serve as grateful symbol of white patronage and black possibility. Praise God that dead colored people were not stupid. Maybe they could not read what their country wrote, but they could certainly read the world around them.

Colin Kaepernick, one learns, was the son of a more recent black-and-white union; raised in the suburbs, he found himself on the football field—that world where excellence of whatever body cannot be denied and hard work pays off whoever you are. It is the positive, feel-good narrative about race and sport, except it is still a narrative about race, the obverse of the claim that would come later in which he was an angry, ungrateful, unworthy *black* man. Maybe he was just a kid who liked, was good at, and worked hard at football.

When you remove the racial frame, he could have been doing any job, and even while kneeling he was speaking as a citizen. Tell me which of those narratives you first believed. Because it is raced, because he is black, his civic speech was censored, as the emperor and his gang went wilding in a pique of mass projection.

One of the things we proclaim when we watch sport is that it is race neutral, one of society's visibly integrated spaces. The reaction to Kaepernick, divided as it was along the race line, shows the fragility of all such claims.

Integration is still a story we *wish to believe*, and never question too deeply: a new form of mass entertainment. In a race-neutral world, that man could speak his mind and be treated as anyone else speaking his mind, with respect or, if athletes are uniquely to be denied the right to express political opinions at work, proportional repercussion. But in contemporary America we are not integrated or race neutral; we are a world of exceptions and, beyond that, color blindness, a form of collective myth, dream-wish, and, when that falls apart, panic.

Kaepernick, who sports an Afro, played in San Francisco, across the bay from Oakland, where the Black Panthers, who popularized the Afro, originally formed.

Their catalyst, as noted, was to protest the 1966 police killing of Matthew Johnson (a young man you've probably never heard of—we only remember the names of the dead who first got to do some living). It was two years after the assassination of Malcolm X. More than fifty years later we are still protesting the murder of unarmed black men. When Kaepernick lent his voice as an athletic hero to this, it incited whiteness to run riot. The NFL's investors capitulated. There was, after all, $16 billion in yearly revenue at stake and 400 million people in need of entertainment.

One of the oft-noted differences between the militant phase of civil rights and the earlier southern phase was that down south, people were marching to be able to vote and in protest of lynching. In the North they wanted more than a bare minimum of rights and protections: the full measure of respect and dignity of citizenship, and, yes, manhood.

When we look at football, we tell ourselves we are watching a level field where excellence is rewarded and we can practice color blindness, ignoring physical difference to recognize only individual greatness, team and tribe. Some of this may well be true (at least when we talk about our own team), but even then there is always the subtext that says "despite being black" (*this one person excelled* or *someone was given a shot*), an exception to real life. When real life intrudes, the field is simply another space to control or silence blackness.

In 2019 the NFL settled with Kaepernick, and his former teammate Eric Reid, out of court for an undisclosed amount, reported to be $10 million. The terms of settlement impose a gag order, so we will never know all the evidence, except the evidence in front of us every weekend in winter.

Football players are warriors. It is why they thrill us and why people like Modell and Trump want so badly to own them and to control them. Like Snyder and his racist media rant in 1988, they all represent the weak man's desire for control through the shelter of the group, which is the opposite of heroic; it's cowardice. But this fear and corruption are protected by and carry forth the narratives of whiteness—even when they ignore it, maybe even especially when they claim to ignore it.

10

HIPSTERS IN THE CITY

Forgive them father for they know not what they do.
—Lauryn Hill, *The Miseducation of Lauryn Hill*

I remember walking to a friend's house near New York's Union Square one day and having the clear, distinct thought of entering colonial space. All the black shops had disappeared. So had a certain kind of black person: the poets, the Carolina folks, the old heads still talking about revolution. Things change in the city, I know. That's part of the charm. You need new stuff, a different kind of food, a good bottle of wine, a fresh suit of clothes. I also happened to like the old stuff just fine: bookstores, soul food, dancing until dawn, cursing out cab drivers the way they do in Rome when someone doesn't stop for the intersection, like cursing is a national sport. The old heads, the ones who told us either we had missed the revolution or they would, used to tell us how different our lives were and how different they weren't. This was back when I was still beginning to understand historical time and thought it was an arrow you rode rather than the sphere that contained you, not both, the same way they try to tell you light may be a particle or a wave. This was before we had computers in our pockets or children on our minds. People change in the city. That part of town had been African and free, in a kind of way at least, since the time it was Dutch; then one day it was just gone. Except the African graveyard they came across when building the new library, and no one knew what to do with all those bones.

How do you combat the invisible? Those things we harbor within without knowing, or that indeed we do not wish to know? In a 2014 experiment, scientists at the University of Chicago discovered that rats possessed empathy, an attribute most commonly thought to be uniquely human, and would free other rats caught in a trap. However, spotted rats helped only other spotted rats, white rats other white rats, black rats other black rats, and so on.

However, rats raised in a cage with those of other physical appearance exhibited no bias. They showed empathy toward the kinds of rats they grew up with regardless of appearance. "In mammals," the authors concluded, "helping is preferentially provided to members of one's own group. . . . We found that rats helped trapped strangers by releasing them from a restrainer, just as they did cagemates. However, rats did not help strangers of a different strain, unless previously housed with the trapped rat. . . . Thus, strain familiarity, even to one's own strain, is required for the expression of pro-social behavior." The study didn't test to find out whether a level of familiarity short of living together fostered the same response or by what age it is too late to develop this response.[1]

In humans, we know subliminal biases are transmitted before language is acquired. "Children pick up cues, starting with faces and going on to absorb the implicit attitudes of their parents," notes Gavin Evans in *Skin Deep*. "These can be hard to dislodge, because even when explicit attitudes change, implicit attitudes can be passed on to succeeding generations by more subtle signals. . . . It is possible that as a result of early childhood experiences, subliminal over-consciousness of race persists."[2] This means that even if a parent *professes* to be nonracist yet *responds* to people of different appearances differently, the child learns to as well. Such attitudes are often changed, however, through the experience of working with people of other backgrounds, being exposed to nonracial ideas, and seeing a diversity of people in positions of power. Words matter, of course, but everyone knows that what kids really learn is what their parents actually do.

It stands to reason that the earlier the intervention to counter this occurs, the better the results. We also know that kids in integrated educational environments have better outcomes but that it's a multigenerational process. In conversations with friends whose lives are more integrated than most, there is always a story about a moment on the playground, a night in the dorm, a ride on the school bus, in which race was directly encountered in an environment of equality and was ultimately understood in a new way, as a thing to both see and see beyond. Watching children on the playground, I see not only how natural it is for them to meet, make friends, and quarrel over toys with no concern for race, but also how the drip of society slowly instills racial poisons into them. Americans do this in the ways they speak of racial difference, in the ways they treat one another, and in the ways the environment itself has been shaped to program and influence this behavior.

We also know some of the results are lethal. According to Harvard sociologist David Williams, one of the foremost scientists on the effects of race, "Decades of research by social psychologists has shown that if you hold a negative view of a group in your subconscious, if you meet a member of that group you will discriminate against that person. You will treat them differently. It's an unconscious process. It is a subtle process, but it occurs among even the most well-intentioned of individuals."[3]

Such is the ingenuity of racial technologies that they hijack the deep interior. However, Williams further notes, research has also found that "residential segregation is the secret source that creates racial disparities in the United States."[4] Where we live is near the root of it all.

For those who live in isolation from other groups, the ideas they form about them are shaped in other environmental ways as well, especially the images they receive though media. In books, newspapers, and magazines the most frequent words associated with black people are *poor, violent, lazy*. The leading adjectives associated with whites are *wealthy, progressive, conventional, successful*.[5]

This explains at least part of the reaction a white police officer may have upon seeing a black man and why the cop's first reaction might be to reach for his gun. It's not just the cop aiming at you, but the world.

In addition to what Stokely Carmichael described as the "overt racism" of premeditated violence and structural segregation that most people can clearly see once they know to look for it, yet another vector of violence follows directly from the institutions we have made or suffered ourselves to live within, which "explains why whites are more discourteous toward blacks, why they fail to see them. This is a measurable form of discrimination itself, and it too leads to death. In the case of discrimination it is a slow accrual in the black body in the form of higher blood pressure, abdominal disease, and premature death."[6]

It is the same problem our friend James Sullivan diagnosed back in the 1700s, "the prejudice which education has fixed in the minds of the white against the black people." This is why he proposed that "being at the same schools etc., with the rising generation that prejudice which has been so long and inveterate against them . . . will be lessened within thirty or forty years."[7] Because of the way that the education system conspired to work against integration, one of the most effective cures has eluded us. So has an even more effective one, simply living around one another.

It isn't that it does not happen at all but that it is happening at a controlled trickle, and, to the extent that encounters across the race line happen later in life, in public spaces, instead of in our homes or in the neighborhoods where we live, it may be happening too late. To the extent we have known the problem and the answer for two hundred years, it should be clear how very late.

Part of the way we hide is in language, a window shade that may raised or drawn to the outside world as well as the interior. Many Americans who move to New York City from other parts of the country cite as one of their primary reasons the city's famous diversity, a real-world United Nations where all are said to meet and mingle like the waters of the oceans.

According to a Brown University study, New York is the fourth most diverse city in the nation. However, its neighborhoods rank as only the forty-ninth most diverse.[8] This means that while there are all kinds of people in the city as a whole, they live in different parts of it. The disparity between how many different groups live in a metropolitan area and how many of them are in the same neighborhood across racial groups tells how segregated the city is. There are people-sized and country-sized factors that cause this, individuals entangled in and re-creating the race line they learned in the cradle in various ways.

One of the main factors is gentrification. As liberally educated suburbanites move to town, they cluster among one another. They claim to move there for "diversity." Their actual behavior is the same apartness they grew up around. For them, diversity is the thrill of many different restaurants and relief from the ennui of sterilized environments, not civic engagement and equal interaction across group lines.

As a trickle of white people move into each successive neighborhood, it becomes commensurately more desirable to other whites, as they see others like them there. As more new people arrive, policing increases, and "magnet programs" for the new kids are created, but also of course racial attraction and repulsion.

Rents begin to increase, and those who just happen to be less well educated and less gainfully employed are priced out. But more importantly gentrification braids into what economists call rent-seeking, a process, often corrupt like bribery, by which value is transferred without being created. The city, by sending in police who are now there to serve and protect and not just stop and frisk, or investing in the schools, or building handsome new bike lanes and green spaces like the new people want, is helping increase value for the new people in ways it did not for the old hands.

The problem would be bad enough starting from an equal playing field among those similarly educated competing for the same jobs and resources. In real life the cost of a mortgage is often offset by an intergenerational loan, which for whites was subsidized generations earlier in the form of government programs. In actuality the problem is not just rent-seeking in the present but compounded rates of return on the asymmetrical investment Uncle Sam made seventy-five years ago in its decisions during the New Deal and after World War II.

A Marxist would say this is a classic example of the ways in which economy, law, and ethics are broken apart under capitalism, the better to exploit people. Marx was right about enough things in the last century, including the last global recession, that his description of the problem seems eerily prescient. However, Marx meant to describe conditions before universal suffrage, under a feudal state, not in a democracy.[9]

As in old Europe the nexus of power and money still doesn't function with equal concern for the interests of all. There were class interests at play, of course, but race even more than class. Four years after Lyndon Johnson signed the Civil Rights Act, Richard Nixon won the presidency largely by appealing to white rage and fear of integration. The efficacy of this platform in winning southern voters has long been understood. Contemporary historians have begun to point out, however, that the appeal wasn't only southern but also fundamentally suburban. The postwar exodus of whites to the suburbs, where they could get FHA mortgages that blacks couldn't, established all-white enclaves that became the norm for generations born long after they understood how such spaces were created. They were being environmentally conditioned, even if their stated politics did not sound like they had much in common with old Dixie: "White flight . . . represented a much more important transformation in the political ideology of those involved. Because of their confrontation with the civil rights movement, white southern conservatives were forced to abandon their traditional, populist, and often starkly racist demagoguery and instead craft a new conservatism predicated on the language of rights, freedom, and individualism," observes Princeton historian Kevin M. Kruse in his 2007 book, *White Flight*. "In their own minds segregationists were instead fighting *for* rights of their own . . . such as the 'right' to select their neighbors, their employees, and their children's classmates . . . and perhaps most important the 'right' to be free from what they saw as the encroachment of the federal government."[10]

It was an effective strategy that still remains unspoken. According to former Nixon chief of staff H. R. Haldeman, Nixon "emphasized that you have to face the fact that the whole problem is really the blacks. The key is to devise a system that recognized this while not appearing to."[11]

As people like Alabama governor George Wallace deployed gross appeals to white supremacy, including collaborating with the Ku Klux Klan to disrupt court-ordered school segregation, white-shoe Republicans began to bore into the language, emphasizing "law and order" and "states' rights," in the same way that revisionist histories of the Civil War insisted it was never about slavery.

Lee Atwater, another influential Republican strategist, has been even more explicit in his depiction of the "Southern Strategy":

> Y'all don't quote me on this. You start out in 1954 by saying, "Nigger, nigger, nigger." By 1968 you can't say "nigger"—that hurts you. Backfires. So you say stuff like forced busing, states' rights and all that stuff. You're getting so abstract now [that] you're talking about cutting taxes, and all these things you're talking about are totally economic things and a by-product of them is [that] blacks get hurt worse than whites. And subconsciously maybe that is part of it. I'm not saying that. But I'm saying that if it is getting that abstract, and that coded, that we are doing away with the racial problem one way or the other. You follow me—because obviously sitting around saying, "We want to cut this," is much more abstract than even the busing thing, and a hell of a lot more abstract than "Nigger, nigger."[12]

George Wallace, who ran as a white nationalist in the 1968 election because he deemed it to be the most effective campaign strategy, carried all the states of the Deep South. Nixon was perceived as a moderate by comparison, although the issues he ran on—states' rights, law and order—were the same. His language was less embarrassing, a more acceptable fig leaf, one that could be embraced by educated suburbanites across the country.

There is a line of transmission from resistance to emancipation in the eighteenth century to resistance to integration in the twentieth. When Nixon ran for reelection in 1972, he carried every state in the nation except Massachusetts.

There is a similarly direct, though less visible, line of transmission from twentieth-century housing policy and politics to the modern American city—subconscious bias shaped by what we read and see, racial isolation in the social and private spheres, encoded public speech, and other kinds of masking behaviors— all representing the most basic forms of racism. But we have been further trained not to simply mask our true thoughts on race, but to deploy compensatory behaviors. Instead of denials, we perform our wokeness or guilt. Often it is simply the conscious mind performing a cover story for the deeper interior, happening as it does on the animal level.

We carry these things with us into spaces we tell ourselves are diverse, from a segregated suburb, to a nominally integrated classroom, into the workplace and our homes in a new city. Often the interactions and conversations that do take place across race lines are simply surface phenomena that allow us to avoid a more damning truth. On the deeper level we are all actors within the overarching racialized system even when we occupy spaces that seem exceptional. In contemporary New York we talk about rich rats and poor rats, black and brown and yellow and white rats, individual effort, and IQ scores. All of these work to cover up the underlying problem, absolve us of collective responsibility, but really keep things the same, because what we say and what we actually do, the way we live, are still miles apart.

When we say "diverse," we mean, of course, not *too* diverse, or perhaps even "temporarily," as the neighborhood is gentrified by an influx of more white people from the suburbs and exurbs, and the existing population is slowly displaced, until it reaches the moment of incline and the process is irreversible.

Former New York City mayor Ed Koch, a Democrat, invited this in the 1980s, calling out to white America for "pioneers" to come east to claim black and brown neighborhoods for civilization. Millions heeded the call, a movement of population the director Spike Lee, a Brooklyn native, has colorfully derided as "Christopher Columbus shit." The individual did not even need to have corrupt intent: if you were white, the policy was rent-seeking on your behalf, diverting value from the old to the new. White over black.

After the Fair Housing Act of 1968, African Americans began to move out of the federally created ghettos into previously unavailable neighborhoods. Starting in 1968, millions of whites fled to the suburbs, ensuring that segregation would continue in a new form.

By the 1990s, the trend of suburbanization began to slowly reverse: in the suburbs themselves, "data shows that as minorities move into suburbs, white families are making small and personal decisions that add velocity to the momentum of discrimination. They are increasingly choosing to self-segregate into racially isolated communities."[13] One of the places they have begun to resegregate is in cities. Whites who had grown up in the suburbs began to see the inner cities as desirable, drawn at first by the creative vibrancy and soon enough by the amenities that were created by the cities for their benefit. By the early twenty-first century many previously black neighborhoods were nearly all white: "When white neighborhoods experience socioeconomic ascent, they retain whites. And when minority neighborhoods experience it, they become more white."[14] When blacks can no longer afford their neighborhoods, it isn't simply a matter of economic inequality, it is both racial and economic inequality. Colonialism by another name. Whites, who had fled the cities to live in racially segregated places for ninety years, brought segregation with them as they returned to the city. But it was no longer called white flight, but rejuvenation, underlining the fact that, to the white mind, the problem is the presence of black people.

In New York City, where the trend of "revitalization," as city planners soon called it, began, special concessions were made to keep the new population from returning to the suburbs. These concessions occurred in education (where zoning and magnet programs served as set-asides for the newbies), in policing (as cops flooded into previously underpoliced neighborhoods and began the practice of stopping young black and brown men on the street to frisk them), and in housing (under a twenty-year reign of conservative mayors, beginning with Rudy Giuliani, elected by the ostensibly liberal population, and continuing under progressive ones). White desire was the same whether it was red or blue. Red people foamed at the lips. Blue people hired Giuliani to turn purple and foam at the lips for them.

New York, the city with the country's largest black population, is now one of the most segregated in the nation. And although the city as a whole has seen its economy grow, the number of black-owned business decreased by over 31 percent between 2000 and 2015, as opposed to a nearly 3 percent increase in the country as a whole. The average yearly wage outside of Manhattan is $21,538. Not only are the gains of the growing economy better for some than others; for black people the new economy is measurably worse.[15]

Politically, the population of New York is avowedly progressive. No Republican president has won New York City (or state) since Calvin Coolidge in 1924. In New York City, Republicans held office from 1994 to 2013, but that includes Bloomberg's full term as an Independent, after he switched parties but not policies. In local elections it did not matter whether the mayor was Democrat or Republican as long as the policies were skewed to reward the new. What we claim our politics to be are abstractions compared to local policies, which strike much nearer to home.

New York's strategic importance to the British was that it was centered midway between the slave bastions of the Caribbean and the free states of New England, where cotton was processed. It was the middleman in the triangular trade, and it has triangulated its attitudes and policies ever since. When Frederick Douglass escaped slavery in Maryland, he spent his first night of freedom as a fugitive on the same West Side wharf where Olaudah Equiano had landed in the city a hundred years earlier, fearful of capture. During the Civil War it was the most pro-Confederate city in the North. Before he fled the city for Europe, not long after a violent outburst in a Greenwich Village bar where he had been refused service, James Baldwin observed that "they walked the same streets I walked, after all, rode the same subways, must have seen the same increasingly desperate and hostile boys and girls . . . they had no right not to know that; if they did not know that, they knew nothing and had no right to speak as though they were responsible actors in their society. . . ."[16] Black people in New York are still being refused service, and white New Yorkers are still pretending not to know it, or else that it is something newly discovered.

The new segregationists employ and respond to the pioneer language of colonialism, as well as the northern version of Nixon's southern strategy—crime, school districts, housing—when venturing into a previously untapped housing market, basking in the jungle-safari feeling of the unknown but also the sense of being progressive and open-minded as they anticipate the return on their investment. On the national level they speak the same language and believe themselves to sincerely mean it, but they cannot talk directly of integration, for when integration meets white self-interest, majority desire joins across the political divide. New York, celebrated for its diversity, is actually many adjacent spaces that sometimes touch, most often transactionally. This is the city that set the trend for other cities to follow.

Follow it they have. An army of college grads listening to rap music, as they shove actual black people aside. It is an ancient enough pattern at this juncture that words, changeable as they are, matter so much less than facts on the ground.

In 1958, 44 percent of whites said they would move if a black family became their next-door neighbor; today the figure is 1 percent. In 1964, 18 percent of whites claimed to have a friend who was black; today 86 percent say they do, while 87 percent of blacks assert they have white friends. At the same time only 40 percent of African Americans consider themselves members of the middle class. While the fraction of black families with middle-class incomes rose almost 40 percentage points between 1940 and 1970, it has increased only another 10 points in the fifty years since then. Attitudes are one thing; policies are another.[17]

What happens? In the 1980s, during the Reagan administration,

> There was a dramatic reversal in federal support for affirmative action. In 1981, the Office of Federal Contract Compliance Programs came under new leadership that was committed neither to the organization nor to affirmative action. In 1982, a fervent opponent of affirmative action, Clarence Thomas, was appointed to head the Equal Employment Opportunity Commission. During the presidency of Ronald Reagan, a serious effort was made to rescind Executive Order 11246, and when that failed, steps were taken to weaken affirmative action enforcement.[18]

Reagan remains a conservative hero. Thomas, of course, is currently on the Supreme Court.

As in education these efforts toward integration were working, but a government hell-bent against them led an increasingly virulent conservative attack until they no longer even bothered to hide their intent, and there arrived a president in open, instead of covert, league with white nationalists, whose language he regularly amplified from the White House. The policies were the same as those of every conservative since Nixon, or Jackson for that matter, but the wink and nudge and fig leaf were gone.

Presidents, however, are reflections of the will of the people, channeling the zeitgeist but not creating it. Donald Trump is not smart enough to invent race, but he has second sight when it comes to using it, tapping a pool of not only vocal racists but also an equal number of ones whose passivity derives from perceived self-interest.

Like most people in America, Trump is repeating the things that formed him, and while he represents something hideous, it is an ugliness that rises from the people and the past. When it comes to where we live and how, that is not a question of liberal and conservative, but black and white, including minorities who assimilate into the systems that buffer whiteness, in hopes it is better to be in on the grift than to be left out.

From without it looks genteel, farmers' markets and lifestyle brands and bike lanes and a never-ending cornucopia of nice things. But the free-range beef, like the promise of abundance first held out to European immigrants, is ranched on land stolen from the people who were there before and are now pushed ever deeper into the wilderness or else onto reservations. It does not matter why or where, so long as it is mentally and geographically offshore.

11

THIS IS US? AMBIVALENCE AND REPRESENTATION

This is why the South is so panic-stricken and indeed
the country is so panic-stricken. It means the generation
of boys and girls sitting at the lunch counters are the first
generation in this country's history who were not controlled by America's image of them.

—James Baldwin, Canadian television interview, 1960

One of the most popular TV shows in recent years, *This Is Us*, depicts a loving couple who, after losing one of their triplets during childbirth, adopt an orphan from the maternity ward to fill the void of their grief. The show's twist is that the third would-be triplet is African American, making the larger social questions of integration a family drama, in which race and racial difference are, like dating, self-acceptance, career setbacks, and other typical plots of network drama, simply another complexity of modern life.

Television, which was invented in the United States, is among the most quintessentially American art forms. Since the inception of the medium, people have recognized its power to create national narratives of America both as it is but far more often as we would have it be. As mass culture, electronic visual media represent a crossroads of the national interior, a place where public life and the stories and symbols that inform our private selves intersect. The examples focusing on race—from *Amos 'n' Andy* to *The Wire*—are no exception.

In *This Is Us*, Randall, the adopted brother, portrayed with understated aplomb by Sterling K. Brown, happens to be academically gifted, scrupulously decent, clean-cut, and handsome. He works as a successful Wall Street trader and, in his domestic life, is a self-sacrificing family man. A character as unobjectionably admirable as any role ever played by Sidney Poitier in the 1960s, when the color line was first contested in mainstream cinema. He is a Barack Obama figure white people *wish* was their friend, or better still their brother, and on the small screen he can be. The colonists in early Virginia would have seen in him the perfect black Englishman.

Randall is such a model minority, in fact, that the only person who has a problem with him is his fictive brother, Kevin, who, in a pique of sibling rivalry, worries he is being universally displaced by black men after an African American is hired to take his place on the successful television show he had helmed. It is a reflection of the feeling he has been supplanted by his darker brother in their mother's affection, but also a sly comment on white insecurity, which the show plays for laughs. At that level of attainment and quarters so close, whatever beef they have is less about race than the two of them.

However improbably, the theme of black children adopted into white families is a television staple. *This Is Us* shares symbolic DNA with earlier shows like *Different Strokes*, which enjoyed a smash run of eight seasons between 1978 and 1985, and *Webster*, also wildly popular, about African American kids adopted into white families. The heritable trait is that in each case it casts the family in question as the white savior of a black orphan.

In the real world the practice of "transracial" adoptions was relatively rare at the time of Randall's fictional adoption, in the mid-1970s. As of 1972, approximately fifty thousand white couples had adopted black children, but the practice soon came under attack, primarily by black social workers who feared the kids would become deracinated and thus ill-prepared to deal with life as black adults in America. In the real world, black people, knowing exactly how many were orphaned, wanted white saviors nowhere near their children.

Randall turned out fine, save the psychological need to be perfect and, modern America being what it is, suffering from a latent anxiety disorder. In addition to insecurities common to the adopted, this need to be perfect represents the burden of expectation. Because as one increasingly understands that the white world is predisposed to judge black people through the negative lens of race, one performs in a way and excels to a degree meant to overcome such biases. Randall may have integrated his gated Westchester community and attained every other spoil of bourgeois success, but he remains unable to integrate himself in a manner that simply allows him to exist, without special explanation or performance. It is a character trait that tells as much about the individual as the larger project of assimilation, a "minority" adjustment to the subconscious conditioning of whites, and one of the ultimate tests of the race line: the freedom to exist within oneself and society without division.

As a metaphor for transcending race, the family drama is an obvious one. But it is also more than metaphor: after all, of the four million people who were emancipated by the Civil War, a million of them are believed to have been of "transracial" parentage. The interrelatedness of Americans across the race line is an uncomfortable fact buried in the national subconscious. Slaves were not only born "in the family"; often they *were* family. The appeal of the premise is in allowing us to explore a psychologically charged issue at safe remove. Catharsis for sin and shame, rejection and guilt.

Besides Randall the *Ubermensch*, the show keeps racial compartments scrupulously neat. There's no interracial dating or friendship in the lives of any of the triplets.[1] The white kids live in a white world, and Randall leads the life of any other affluent Afro-Saxon, albeit in isolation.

The one significant time there is traffic across traditional lines of race, with its implicit destabilization, is when Randall's adoptive mother, Rebecca (Mandy Moore), sleuths out his biological father, William (Ron Cephas Jones), taking the bus across town to find him. They are united by mutual concern for Randall's well-being, and through this are able to see one another. They maintain a correspondence over the years, which Rebecca hides from Randall, who discovers as an adult that she knew who his biological father was all along, and hid it from him. In its vigilant nosiness, its protectiveness, its well-meaning fallibility, it isn't only insecurity over losing her child but a perfectly maternal act. Who but a parent *could* do something to you so messed up?

Following a strange man across the tracks to an unknown part of town to confront a threatening figure serves as a classic chthonic transformation ritual: Orpheus or Persephone in the underworld, Jesus rising from the dead. In Rebecca's case the phase shift isn't from mortal to god, but stranger to kin. She has crossed a forbidden boundary, not of life and death, but of race. There will be other moments of cross-cultural awkwardness to navigate and insider information transmitted, but this is when she becomes not only guardian but mother.

The reason William had abandoned his son is that he suffers a drug addiction and is unable to care for his boy. Randall's adoptive father and brother also have addiction problems with alcohol. It would be impossible for Randall to deal with the fear of being unloved or not belonging by turning to drink or drugs, or even a therapist. Instead, he "self-corrects" when faced with adversity, stuffing it all back inside.

Randall's backstory is that his greater challenge is not to be accepted by whites but the need to find the spiritual fix he needs from the black world. He accomplishes this by choosing black friends, marrying a black woman, and taking a road trip to Memphis with his biological father, where the two make peace with each other and old-timey black culture.

Soon afterward he furthers the connection by deciding to foster the hardest-of-luck children, a preteen girl who brings with her every problem black America is said to be beset by. He wishes to honor his dead biological father, his deceased adoptive father, but really to plug his suburban soul into the socket of the great black world to save and be saved by it. He is seeking an authentic self.

In all other respects his is a life of assimilation into white norms. He's the exceptional black man, now attending to the problems of the black community. For the show's white characters their own individual needs are paramount in a way Randall's can never be, because as the black person in the white world, but also as one of a handful of blacks privileged to cross the racial divide, he is still as much symbol as man.

There is only one occasion when his Ubermensch persona cracks: under intense pressure at home, he doesn't manage to properly prepare for an important work meeting. Instead of asking for or hiring help, he decides to wing it. His lack of preparation becomes apparent during the meeting, and one of his colleagues, an Asian American, steps up with the necessary information, the model minority now usurping his place at the table. Randall subsequently loses the account, an effective demotion. It is a one-strike rule that he has internalized: there is no room for imperfection.

In the wake of this he realizes a series of small slights from his boss over the years: failure to remember an allergy, small things forgotten. The discourtesy may or may not be racial in nature. Certainly it is not a charge Randall would make in public; after all, the entire point of your life has been to prove you can excel without crutches. Of course there is a racial undercurrent, the element of contingency, the discount on your achievement, but you know how to deal with it.

His demotion serves as a catalyst for him to claim his true worth, which he does by quitting his job. He is right to leave, of course, but as a plot point it is hard to believe, because telling

the man what's on your mind and quitting in a blaze of glory—
what with two kids, a wife who works as a homemaker, and a
mortgage—is an emotional act, and the black Ubermensch is a
figure of emotional discipline. He must be or else risk activating
the rat-level race stereotypes his persona is built to defeat. No
wonder the man suffers from anxiety attacks.

If *This Is Us* bends over backward in its need to portray African
Americans in a noble light (albeit with an indirect criticism), it
is because of the cultural context in which it exists. The history
of film and television is a history of incessantly negative stereotypes of African Americans.

Nor do these stereotypes belong to the primordial past. One
of the most influential shows in what has come to be known as
the second golden age of television is the turn-of-the-century
cable hit *The Sopranos*, which, along with *The Wire*, introduced
postmodern relativism to the small screen: a set of techniques
by which absolutes and authority are questioned, including the
authority of narrative itself (asking the reader/viewer to question
all claims of truth and authority in the world). In practice this
interrogation may be profound enough to transform societies or
shallow as a puddle in a fig leaf.

After all, stories, like the cultural belief systems they are entwined with, are infinitely malleable. Just as we are always transmitting and receiving subtle cues that maintain the dominant
narrative, we can always share or receive one powerful enough to
affect the culture as a whole, transforming us and the world.

At its best *The Sopranos*, which bills itself as the most crit-
ically acclaimed television series ever, exhibits a self-referential

knowingness, rooted in film history, psychoanalysis, and deconstructionist theory, all wielded to question the limits of our ability to fully know and change the self and the fictions we weave around ourselves to cope. Whenever it encounters race, however, all such sophistication breaks down into a "nigger nigger" level of primordial crudeness.

The show is famously about a mob boss in northern New Jersey who seeks therapy for his midlife panic attacks. It is set in the upper-middle-class enclave of Short Hills, and much of its narrative verve rises from the inherent tension between bourgeois family life and the norms of the Mafia world, but also the tropes of Mafia movies. The boss, Tony (James Gandolfini), is in analysis but can't stop killing. It's how he provides.

The gangsters all reference classic gangster films and at times imagine themselves in them. Life's imitation of art and art's desire for authenticity are among its central leitmotifs. In this setup the mainstream audience gets to be both voyeur and critic. *The Sopranos* is most brilliant at having its cake and eating it too, which is, of course, the greatest American fantasy: to reconcile violent acts with a virtuous facade and aspirations.

In its analytical worldliness about modern identity politics and the antiquated gender dynamics of the show, Carmela (Edie Falco), Tony's wife, proclaims, "I'm not a feminist . . . but it's the twentieth century," as she attempts to get her husband to allow her a more active role in family decision making. She goes to work as a real estate investor but also clandestinely begins to invest the cash bundled around the house in legitimate financial instruments. It is one of many episodes in which the show entwines normative middle-class values with Mafia codes of conduct to telegraph both the tension between the two and its own sophistication about its endeavor.

Another example of this self-reflective nostalgia occurs in an episode about Columbus Day, in which the plot balances Italian pride with a politically correct interrogation of the violent, racist legacies of the colonization of the American continent. It argues the evidence and points of view for both sides, and the Italian claim is ultimately vanquished by the cultural sensibilities of the twenty-first century, which the Sopranos, save for Tony's job, represent.

All of this breaks down in the face of blackness, most often depicted in the form of gangbangers or junkies who have taken over the neighborhood where Tony's parents once lived, which, if it's like most inner cities in North Jersey, was fled en masse after the 1969 Newark riots. The entire clockworks, the deeper patterns of the show, falter and break as the plot strikes race. A form of blindness that America carves out everywhere around the subject, including the show's critical audience.

The most significant black presence arrives when Meadow Soprano, Tony's daughter, matriculates at Columbia University and begins dating a classmate, Noah Tannenbaum, the son of an African American mother and Jewish American father. Aside from that, he's a film nerd from Los Angeles who in less racist hands, given the show's geometry, might be a natural stand-in or alter ego for the show's creator. One would be most interested in what he would have to say about the narrative he has been cast in and what that conveys.

After their first meeting, Tony takes Noah aside to explain to the young man why he can't date Meadow, expecting Tannenbaum to understand. Apparently it's still not the twenty-first century where interracial dating is concerned, either in the mob or some parts of Short Hills. Tony then begins to play the character's ethnicity for broad comedy, calling him Jamal Ginsburg and insinuating that he got into Columbia only because of affirmative action. In a subsequent scene one of the younger Italian American gangsters finds his romantic advances toward Meadow rebuffed and vigorously protests: "You'd date the black guy but not me." It does not matter that Tannenbaum is an Ivy League student and son of a successful Hollywood lawyer; he is assumed to be unworthy because he is a blackamoor, an assumption that goes unchallenged, aside from Meadow's protest. Tannenbaum has no voice in the matter.

Meadow continues dating Noah until he breaks it off; soon after his father takes the pair to dinner and she describes her own father's occupation as "in the sanitation business." It is the least realized story arc of the entire series. Not only does it fail to fit the pattern that makes the show successful, but it also fails its characters, missing the true embedded tension for a couple like Meadow and Noah. In the real world his parents would caution him he has too much at stake to get mixed up with someone like her, and Noah would be devoted enough to his father to obey. In the real world he has that which she does not but most deeply craves: legitimacy. The inverse of Othello.

I'm not the first person to point out the show's problems with race, which don't seem to affect its critical regard, for most television critics are not only white but also whites without any more than superficial awareness of race in America, or worse, they only recently discovered it.

The show's creator, David Chase, has defended his portrayals of black characters as verisimilitude, even though as a writer and showrunner he otherwise takes his verisimilitude with a grain of salt and self-awareness. When Carmela accuses Tony of sexism, it's funny, and he is eventually forced to relent. When Meadow accuses him of racism, his views never change, which may well be the true verisimilitude. You have to live with your wife, but you don't have to live with black people. Casual racism is performed in ways that aren't questioned in a show that asks the viewer to question everything. It is the blind spot that betrays his art, but a blind spot in artistic representations to which we have long grown inured.

When asked about depictions of race in his work, Chase gave a revealing answer in describing his own upbringing: "How do I explain this? There was, and is, a thing called 'casual racism.' There's not really a lot of hatred involved. It's just not knowing the other and not trusting them. It's plenty racist, but it's not the white-sheet kind of racism. . . . 'Those people are lesser than you; those people don't belong with us; watch out for them.' They never told me any of that stuff. It's just that some of the language and attitudes were such that: They are trying to take away what we have, or live off of our hard work. Things like that."[2] This is, as we have seen, exactly how racism works.

Chase deserves credit, one supposes, for his honesty. But it is truth without reconciliation. He reveals the false reasoning by which liberals hold themselves and society as a whole to a uniquely low standard in matters of race. The white-sheet kind of racism and the casual kind are a continuum of the same thing. One wishes to claim your life all at once. The other bit by bit until you have five fewer years on average; the casual racism that informs the subconscious that, even without being repeated, gets transmitted in decision making across all areas of society, generation over generation. It's what the cop hears without knowing right before he pulls the trigger.

Chase reveals the private space in American life, memories of the past that inform whiteness in the present. But it isn't inert; it still acts on this moment and the future. It is still being re-created and transmitted. Because of unexamined "verisimili-tude," the past pulls itself forward, using Chase as host to rep-licate itself in his own subconscious and in the subconscious of those watching. As one of the most beloved narratives of recent culture, *The Sopranos* affects in turn another generation.

This is the cultural inheritance that few people discuss in public, which is where discussions of race reckoning are usually held, because to talk about it is not only copping to your own inner rat; it's also ratting out your family.

As Edward Said observed,

> Imperialism consolidated the mixture of cultures and identi-ties on a global scale. But its worst and most paradoxical gift was to allow people to believe that they were only, mainly, exclusively, white, or Black, or Western, or Oriental. Yet just as human beings make their own history, they also make their cultures and ethnic identities. No one can deny the per-sisting continuities of long traditions, sustained habitations, national languages, and cultural geographies, but there seems no reason except fear and prejudice to keep insisting on their separation and distinctiveness, as if that was all human life was about. Survival in fact is about the connections between things.[3]

In Chase's case, as well as for so many white Americans, psy-chological survival is still about clinging nostalgically to the invented boundaries of whiteness and tribe. The stakes are meaningful because of the extent to which representation—the stories we are told and images we see about who we are and what this world is—shapes our individual selves and potentialities of society as a whole. Television alone cannot *fulfill* these potentialities, of course; no single realm can.

In culture, as in law and business, we are still in what might optimistically be called a transitional state, and more negatively a collective cover-up to hide what the past creates in the here and now.

The way I've always read W. E. B. Du Bois's famous line about the racial veil is that we can also measure how far society has progressed or failed in the degree to which the African American experiences self-consciousness in relationship to the rest of society. How vigilant must the Negro feel they have to be about how they are seen—their own skin—in public, in private, in their own mind in order to navigate society? How much can you live your own interior dream and the self that rises from that, and how much are you trapped in someone else's fiction?

These are questions not only about how much race affects material experience but also the deep levels of being. The real race line isn't what you can see and touch but what's inside us that can't be actualized or individuated.

Dear White People probes this indirectly in the context of Winchester University, a fictitious Ivy League school where most of the students believe themselves to be post-racial. This fiction explodes when a black woman of mixed parentage named Samantha broadcasts a controversial campus radio show called *Dear White People.*

This television series, though didactic at times, draws out the unequal treatment experienced by the African American students, in matters large and small, because of race even in one of the most educated and privileged of spaces. It further explores not simply white presumption and offense but also the shields that progressives stand behind to deny the attitudes, vanities, and presumptions that they carry about and project onto black people. If the black kids are less impressed than the white kids, it is because they know something about America the whites do not, and know further about the veil that functions not only to divorce black people from themselves but also to separate white people from the reality of what's going on.

In the show's pilot the school humor magazine decides to host a blackface party, which has been, in fact, a resurging phenomenon on college campuses in recent years, but we are now supposed to accept it as being, you know, ironic. The planners claim that their reason for throwing the party is in response to the provocations of Sam's show, which they call reverse racism. It's a knotted premise, but the episode slowly takes apart the new knot of language people employ, like the claim of verisimilitude or states' rights, to ward off the charge of being complicit with the racist past that produced us.

In this case the distancing mechanism is the claim of parody. Those who wish to expose the subterfuge hack into a computer because the language enveloping the white characters is so accomplished that it can be exposed only by trespassing into private space. At some point language breaks down into shadow. If consciousness is hidden from us after all, and our attempts to understand it often prove untrustworthy, then so much more do our words.

The show is further concerned with the multitude of strategies African Americans employ to navigate such spaces and assert or maintain their own agency (as opposed to the narratives of whiteness) as its conspicuously beautiful cast otherwise comes of age in America. Its archetypes—rich kids, poor kids, middle-class kids, militant kids, weird kids, conformists, geeks—are all world-beaters, but whenever they encounter the white kids around them, they are foremost black kids, measured, accepted, rejected, tolerated according to how they conform to white needs and expectations.

The black kids know this, of course, as black people do, and are engaged actively or passively with ignoring, subverting, overcoming, enduring, abolishing, obliterating the race line.

It is a more complex question than mere assimilation. The students are aware of their own privileged access but further aware that blacks have been assimilated into American culture since it was a colony, and have made seminal contributions to all aspects of American life ever after. On what terms should they further assimilate?

The black kids are engaged in joining the institutions of power, institutions that once excluded them and now offer them entrance at a cost. What *they* want is to access the full richness and opportunities of the world without erasing themselves as black people, a project that the black middle class has been engaged in for eons. There are a multitude of avenues, but like all paths, the one you take is deeply personal in ways that maybe only other black people see and understand.

The show's archetypal characters embody the range of answers—the middle-class kids trying on strident rhetoric, the hyper-assimilated overachiever, the ghetto genius, the rebels from all walks of life who actively question their terms of belonging in America, what it will cost them, and who they must be—and in the process display a vaster range of blackness than

we usually see on screen. However, as 5 percent of the population of the university, the characters are never free of the white
gaze and the need to disprove, deconstruct, or otherwise combat
the presumptions of liberal whiteness as its bearers, equally pre-
cocious, disavow their existence.

What many of them face is a question of how far they wish
to bend to accommodate a system that feels it has done enough
by granting them access to such learned community and privilege. Their place among the best has been vouched by virtue of
being there. The rest is up to them, which seems mostly right
until a cop pulls a gun on one of the black students. What it
stands for in the show is the encoded kind of racism, the casual,
clueless, but no less lethal effects that race produces every day
by people who inadvertently measure themselves according to
where they are on the spectrum of racism instead of justice.

The inventors of race fled the scene long ago, but its machinery keeps running in the background. Because it is socially
frowned upon, people have learned to perform their disdain.
But to think one deserves special credit for not being racist
points back to the false measures we live by. It's how you are
supposed to be. The students at Winchester represent those
who have defied the machinery working against them at every
turn until that point, but those around them see them as proof
the machinery has been disassembled. When it reveals itself on
campus, the question becomes existential: how to protect your
life as an individual against the larger apparatus of a society in
which you also function as a symbol. As the show's title, *Dear
White People*, suggests, the key to understanding the symbol is
rarely your own.

Earn, the character played by Donald Glover in the cable series *Atlanta*, would fit easily among the characters on *Dear White People*. Instead, he has dropped out of Princeton and returned to the working-class neighborhood where he grew up in order to pursue an entrepreneurial career in music management. He breached the Ivy League race line but has decided to return. He is struggling by all measures until a mix tape his cousin recorded under the nom de guerre Paper Boi (Bryan Henry) starts to gain traction on the streets, and Earn is afforded the opportunity to manage Paper Boi's rapidly rising career.

We never learn why Earn has left Princeton. It might be read as critique or ambivalence about the world of elite universities, an embracing of paths beyond the confines of the ivory tower, or choosing to live in a black world instead of a white one. Whatever it is, Earn—who, in addition to dropping out of college, has a child by a woman with whom he is not in a committed relationship, through no fault on her part; who has assumed career responsibilities that are over his head; and who doesn't seem to be taking any steps to further educate himself—definitely has a chip on his shoulder. Whatever it is—fear of failure, fear of success, fear of full commitment—it is within inches of being the factor that determines his life.

One clue lies in the show's preoccupation with the notion of authenticity. As his career expands, Paper Boi, who supplements his income by selling weed, faces the question of where his loyalties lie, who is loyal to him, and which mode of life to choose.

Earn's own life crosses between the mainstream, both white and black (Atlanta has the most affluent African American population in the country), and the streets from which the music rises.

Whenever *Atlanta* enters into the white world, it depicts a place of especial falseness and crosses immediately into parody. However he may feel about it, though, Earn is a Princeton man—one of Paper Boi's friends, newly released from prison and seeking a job, asks Earn how best to talk to white people—and in the world of the streets he doesn't have much cred. His role is to help his cousin navigate from the hip-hop underground to mainstream success without losing touch of who he is, something Earn is still trying to yoke together for himself.

In addition to the lines between black and white, *Atlanta* moves among the various black worlds of the city, using a deft touch of satire to treat the upper-middle-class black world as nearly identical to the white world. Both seek to embrace Earn, striver that he is, as one of their own, and both represent success, but authenticity belongs to the streets and by extension to the people who inhabit them. The desire of the moneyed world is for the music; they would just as soon leave the people behind.

Another clue to Earn's challenge is his affect, the persona he projects to the world. Whether talking to his parents, a room of criminals, the guests at a cocktail party, a corporate meeting, or at home, Earn is always the same. The surroundings change, but he does not switch codes to better fit into each. Nor is he the only such figure in the show. Darius (Lakieth Stansfield), Paper Boi's partner in the cannabis trade, is a gangster with epicurean tastes and esoteric interests. He is Earn's most frequent foil and interlocutor, an inverse of Earn. Darius belongs comfortably to the world of the street with, aside from his sartorial tastes, a gentleman's milieu and range of interests.

Both Earn and Darius are outlaw figures. They belong neither to the stereotypes of race nor to self-conscious efforts to counter them. Whatever they do—succeed, fail, act responsibly or less so—redounds to them alone, not all the black people in the country. However, in the show's eyes, full selfhood is available only in the black world. Beyond the white and whitened gaze, Earn and Darius inhabit a black interior, comfortable and in active search of its own full self.

It is no coincidence that they live in a context of creativity, where who you are in your deep interior and how you manifest that are as real as the things you own. It is an actualization historically available only to the cultural outlaw, on the thin edge of space, the margins of the world, beyond race.

In the mid-twentieth century the writer Ralph Ellison used the complex metaphor of invisibility to capture the plight of black America. The Invisible Man's cage and burden are not simply that people look *through* him but that when they look *at* him, no one sees who he is, only what they are conditioned or desire to see. The reflection of what they think a black man is, or need him to be, in order to prop themselves up in the racialized world.

The Invisible Man's problem is not that doors do not open; it is that they open only on terms that allow others to capture him. Everything has a cost, of course, but as we learn again and again from Goethe to the blues, the self is always too high a price to pay.

Ellison ends his novel with the protagonist fleeing underground, in search of refuge, as protest, to tunnel to the other side, as the only way to escape a world in which all avenues available to him are modalities of race. When race informs everything and everyone, the only escape is to move beyond its boundaries. Unless we all intend to go underground to escape, the only practical solution is to integrate, including all that has come before. We have only begun to glimpse what that looks like, but we have seen enough to know it is possible, and it has left us afraid.

There are fitful moments of individual communication and symbol that do not ascend to the larger group, whether black or white, because on the individual level one may push race aside momentarily to see the exceptional, or on the symbolic level to see what we need to see. On the whole, though, we know the assembled forces of resistance remain most powerful and entrenched, asking us the question from the threshold: Do we have the courage and faith to go the rest of the way?

Part III

IN LIGHT OF THE *WHITE LION*

As James Baldwin asked: What advantage is there in being integrated into a burning house?

> —Martin Luther King Jr., NBC interview eleven months
> before his assassination

A t an event in midtown Manhattan honoring the late Supreme Court justice and former NAACP attorney Thurgood Marshall, I found myself seated next to a heavyset man
in his early seventies whose face radiated with the clarity that
begins to show, plain as a Lutheran church, in those who have
lived lives of contemplation and purpose. He reminded me of a
Luo chief I once knew.

In the course of the evening I learned he was a Connecti-
cut lawyer who, as a student at Brown, had been instrumental in the campus protests that flared around the country in the
1960s when young people demanded greater societal change in
matters of race, class, and foreign policy. They were turning the

principles and goals of the civil rights movement into direct, local action, calling governments and institutions to account for
their policies, opening previously closed doors, changing the
country. Even if it has become a fashion to second-guess their
organizational structures, they were operating on a scale never
before seen and doing so without much banked, institutional
knowledge and experience to draw from.

As I talked to him, I was reminded how near the civil rights
movement, both the problems it addressed and the sacrifices
made, remains. If I seldom thought about it in the course of
daily life, it is because I was fortunate to be born a generation
later, into a more capacious country. It is a country that is nevertheless still only half-made.

I once thought continuing social change was a matter of inevitability until I realized how little separates my own time from
my parents' and grandparents' generations. I realized as I spoke
to him how much I had convinced myself of this from near-
sightedness, but also for the perfectly simple, selfish reason that
such knowledge reminds us of prior claims on our life, our time,
our comfort.

"If anything," the gentleman next to me said calmly, after I asked his opinion of current affairs, "the racists have
gotten more sophisticated. Now they use algorithms, voter da-
tabases, and an army of billionaires in their cause," an unbroken
line from the preindustrial past to the technological, media-
saturated present. It is not simply the canniness of our enemies
but our own assumptions that tempt us to dismiss the treach-
erous past as settled and gone, and its effects in the present as
matters that will right themselves once enough people are un-
hitched from ignorance. We cling to these views even as the

technologies of this time become new instruments of the same forces. As do the stories we tell ourselves and one another in both public and private, where the things we suppress in order to move smoothly through the world, or that society suppresses so that *it* may move smoothly, exert hidden influence on our every interaction. It is tempting to say "even in the twenty-first century," as people have been saying since the twentieth century, but we are never so sophisticated or as advanced as we believe ourselves to be.

These quantum private realities, the things that have shaped us, are as relevant as the more visible forces of law, government, and finance. Both public experience and private experience are called on when we ask the question, which has been asked before and which I believe desperately needs to be asked outright at this moment in America: Can a society such as ours ever be fully whole?

It is a question we do not ask often or loudly enough, even though history planted it in American soil so uniquely at the beginning of the Republic that wise observers saw that the greatest adversary of American democracy was already internal. "As soon as it is admitted that the whites and the emancipated blacks are placed on the same territory in the situation of two foreign communities," to repeat de Tocqueville's wise observation, "it will be readily understood that there are but two chances for the future: the Negroes and the whites must either wholly part or wholly mingle . . . fortune has brought them together on the same soil, where, although they are mixed, they do not amalgamate, and each race fulfils its destiny apart."[1] We have been standing in that future for some time, answering sometimes one way and sometimes the other. I am not counting those whose answer is reliably negative, but what I believe to be the majority of Americans, who are mixed in their hearts and actions and whose answer cannot be relied upon at all. Those who say one thing and whose lives are in league with another.

We were four hundred thousand when we made landfall, four million on the eve of Emancipation, and a nation of forty-four million today. A number near the population of Spain and so truly a nation within a nation. But one that was here a year before the Pilgrims and, I imagine, will "go back where we came from," as some have recently requested of some of us, exactly one flight before theirs.

Culture shifts whether anyone wishes it to do so or not. Somewhere in all of this history everyone became, or is now in the process of becoming, something apart from what they were before: Americans. The challenge ahead is surmounting the past and what it made, without running from it, to claim full possession of the present and future. The problem is a crack in the *core* of democracy, which is destined to fuse or else break.

However clearly this was diagnosed from the beginning, trying to imagine a wholly mingled future from the center of a slave state was nearly impossible, except for those with the fullest faith in democracy, who believed "the gradual development of the principle of equality is a providential fact. . . ."[2] This providential question was answered most fully by the Civil War or was supposed to have been. Instead, it remains of burning relevance 150 years later because the craven formula of race has poisoned each epoch in America before and after.

The work of righting the nation, titled as it is from the spirit level, has been taken up in four distinct phases.

The first was Emancipation, after the crack in the foundation finally gave way, despite every white liberal attempt to appease it, four score and seven years after founding.

The second, when the dead were buried, was enfranchisement with the full rights of citizens that had been denied ever since the racial slave state was constructed and codified in the eighteenth century, complete with all the stereotypes we know to this day. This was a product of avarice, sloth, wrath, pride, all the sin—if the word retains any meaning—there is, but not destiny.

The third phase, almost exactly a hundred years after Emancipation, was legal *desegregation* of both the formal and informal institutions by which we govern our lives, which had been allowed to fester as quiet liberal racism joined its more outspoken southern counterpart to strip away the rights that war had not *granted* but *restored*.

The ways the country changed at each step would have been, in fact had been, politically impossible for the generations before. But the full measure has always been the one that slipped from the reach of the revolutionary generation. It was advocated most eloquently by Frederick Douglass, a viewpoint that Abraham Lincoln came to share. It was begun and aborted after the Civil War, as the Confederacy and its northern sympathizers managed to have their way again, until the civil rights generation. It was begun again and stalled again under the same attack by the same counterrevolutionary forces. The goal has always been full integration. And it must be our goal now, in our fourth phase of this Republic, which is divided by the same forces. But not, I believe, the people themselves. Civil rights was a mass effort, impossible for any single faction, but a focused coalition with clear goals, impossible to defeat. The strides made during the civil rights generation were mighty, so perhaps we only needed a pause to catch our collective breath. For most of us it was not our victory, however. Those born afterward enjoyed a measure of the freedom possible in this nation largely because of the work of others. We have yet to make our own lasting contribution—dedicated to the underlying global principle, not merely this symbolic take or that glaring atrocity—to this generation-over-generation endeavor, and so we have yet to achieve its fullness and promise. There is nothing wrong in assuming the worst, that this is an impossible task. In fact, historical behavior, and the conceits of our alleged liberal allies, demand any sober-minded person to assume the worst of them—white people, whatever their avowed beliefs, will always corrupt justice and reason to suit their own self-interest and self-regard. Despite this I, defiantly perhaps, believe, as did the Founders, a great deal more is possible, that the unique mission of Americans is to eradicate oppression from the earth. Or at least from the United States. We may either fulfill or betray this mission, but that is the only thing that sets us apart or potentially unites us.

We have now learned enough from the first stages of this experiment—which is what the policies of the Civil Rights Act were, an experiment—to have proof that many of the specific programs work but also incontrovertible proof that white resistance across political ideologies is profoundly invested in halting those programs. Whites are too self-interested to care or else too blind or weak before the tyranny of race to be relied upon. In a country where individual pursuit of happiness and the social contract have been divorced along the lines of race, only integration, which must mean not only the idea of equality and symbolic gestures toward it but also equality of opportunity, solves the problems of race and, in tandem with it, the problems of our incomplete democracy.

We know the country is a better, richer place for the gains we have made so far through collective effort. But the *rate* of change stalled dramatically, and in fact began to reverse, in the 1980s, when the Right waged an effort of massive covert resistance that continues to this day, now in plain sight for all to see, asking nothing but fables to cover itself. The Left obliges it in its politics, in media, in culture, in the privacy of our homes, where we tell our children similar fictions while orienting their lives by the compass of race, and so pulling our own fear and appeasement into the hearts of another generation.

If we wish to go beyond this, in a moment when the problems and rhetoric of white nationalism have found new purchase, and it is a real question how many of us do, we must redouble the efforts to integrate American society on a scale that will encompass all. When I say "all," I include the 30 percent of African Americans who continue to live in a poverty we do not see or else pretend that they chose. On a scale that will address the wage gap. On a scale that will close the education gap. On a scale that will return the lost years in life expectancy. On a scale that will make this society a full democracy, in which the full potentialities of the greatest number of people, regardless of their bodies, are a real priority, not the unearned vanity and insatiable greed of those whose only dream is their own soft comfort and security from the truth of this world. On a scale that makes this half-made nation a full country.

We have achieved enough to know all of these things are perfectly possible and within reach, and frightening as hell for many who have invested so deeply in tools meant to negate the rest of humanity. They have been spectacularly successful at this and so continue the same course, working in ways neither they nor we fully realize, deep inside the body and woven through so much of the history we can see that one has to go back centuries to gain a clear view of the world before this nerve toxin was invented, or else one may negate it by *acting* in ways counter to its intent. What you say does not matter. You are not a reliable narrator of your life. What matters, as in any real endeavor, is the devotion of your behavior.

The traditional political center does not recognize this for the full-blown crisis that it is because the axis is black people. They believe once the gross threat is removed, things will return to normal, invested as they are in the national myth. They do not understand they are in fact the problem, have always been the problem. They are the grazing sheep whose ambling gait, head to the grass, determines the rate of progress.

This holds true across party lines. When white Americans imprison black Americans in greater numbers than any other people anywhere in the world, or deny them decent schools, or try to take away health care, or create permanent ghettos, or lock them out of opportunity and then claim to have a debate on what exactly the problem is and how to fix it, this enacts a charade with a simple bipartisan understanding that there is something wrong with black people—a claim white Americans made across party lines for centuries—and not what is so glaringly obvious. This is the lie that binds whiteness together. It is a self-serving narrative of deceit and cowardice. It is a narrative that serves the white self and not this country. All of these things are, in part, what I mean when I say that the problem of the twenty-first century is the problem of integration.

The generations now finding full political voice are the first in this country to be born after the abolition of legal segregation. The problem now reaches us to consider.

After the assassinations and after the fires, conservative political and religious leaders began to attack the restoration of rights that began in the civil rights years themselves. Progressive white America ignored this, until it actively joined in blaming black America for all the ways whiteness tried to halt this march.

This is the political map and calculus we live by today. Worse: the current political, moral, cultural, economic, and psychological state in America is one in which we claim smug victory in symbolic half-measures and declare that the greater problems of race, really a problem of white supremacy, are insolvable or simply a matter of time. Those who seek office, and a media made up of an army of people whose lives are an undistinguished path from one segregated bubble to the next and who have not even managed to call a presidential election in twenty years, presume to tell us the country is still not ready to complete the task of democracy, helping to ensure that the problems spiral to the next generation.

The historical evidence and patterns are clear: as the counterrevolutionary forces subvert the goal of a fully democratic society, their tools are always false logic, flattery of their own vanity, bribery, threats of violence. Race is the ingenious technology that underlies and powers the entire enterprise by

creating a nation-sized exception to reason, law, morality, emo-
tion, humanity. It is the crook in the arrow of history. It governs
whom we live among, where we go to school, the work we do. It
reaches into our thoughts, often without our knowing, whether
in public, in private company, or alone with ourselves.

Integration is the only frame great enough to encompass
and undo the totality of this harm. It is the only frame that does
not contain the bias of the speaker, and it is the proper field for
our current debates about America and the future of democracy.
Everything else is a derivative of European ethno-nationalism.

By shifting the discussion to integration instead of race, we
shift focus from the past to defining clear, honest goals for the
future. We can measure them, we can manage them, we can
learn from the process, inclusive of the false turns already taken.
But we have to agree what justice looks like, or we will be always
inching toward it, declaring every step a heroic victory, when
really we are inside the labyrinth. The minotaur still waits.

In a just society, people will receive the same education. In
a just society, black people will receive the same social contract
white people do, including the New Deal. In a just society, black
labor will no longer be valued as worthless. In a just society, the
wage gap will be closed. In a just society, people will not be displaced from their homes, as they are with forced evictions in
every neighborhood in this country under gentrification. In a
just society, police will not be incentivized, juries will not be
rigged, and companies will not be paid to engineer a prison
state. In a just society, there will be differences in outcomes, but
they will be individual and they will not trace the path of race.

But instead, in this society, as Thurgood Marshall remarked
shortly before his death, in the years after the victories of the

civil rights movement there was "a deliberate retrenching of civil rights. In the past thirty-five years or more we have truly come full circle. We are back where we started . . . the important question now is where the civil rights struggle should go from here."[3]

Twenty-five years after this observation, fifty years after the Civil Rights Act, we have once again come to one of the sporadic moments of crisis in American society, in which the falseness we like to think of as relegated to the past makes itself undeniably felt, reaching such an amplitude that it has become commonplace to compare the state of national life to a new civil war. But as those who have studied the Civil War know only too well, that is only because the conflagration did not end when the armies went home. We are not in a new Civil War. We are in an old one that was never finished. The anger, fear, and conditioning of the national past are gnawing to reassert themselves in what we imagine to be a more enlightened present, which will never be more enlightened, can never be more enlightened, so long as we continue to re-create the habitat of racism.

In all of this, of course, black people suffer most as the doomed center tries to tell them to be patient again, or progressives perform racial awakening for the umpteenth time, that the long arc of history bends toward justice, that demographics will be the tide to lift the nation out of compromise. Integration asks the same empirical question of everyone, whatever their position in this implausible machine: How long?

Another year? Another generation? Two? Three?

Liberals still cling to an accommodationist myth of post-racialism, a magical maneuver whereby after fifty brief years and a few cloaking words, we have surmounted the past by merely being aware of it and spending half a minute of time in a world that looks, on its surface, only like liberal America's vision of diversity, but not like America itself. The fantasy is accompanied by slogans of inclusion and periodic declarations of being allies in the struggle, instead of allies in the goals. They celebrate yesterday's labor, how far we have come, and how well we all mean, instead of focusing clearly on the journey before us. How long?

By allowing *some* black people access to the full rights of citizenship, liberals protect their own institutions as being just, trusting that more meaningful change will trickle down to the fifteen million living in poverty, or the millions more in abysmal jobs, or the hundreds of thousands in prison. How long?

Conservatives hold to an idealized myth of the past, in which the Civil War did not happen, nursing their grievance against the remembrance of their original apartheid state. Better to double down on this imaginary past instead of a future of redemption. How long? Until your grandfathers are dead? Your mothers? You? Your children? Your grandchildren? Never? One can compel half the nation to agree with anything at all in the name of race, including things any American would find preposterous in any other context whatsoever. How long?

Both points of view, liberal and conservative, are equally self-soothing worldviews that seek at bottom to compartmentalize and avoid the challenges, the difficult work of integration, while absolving white Americans from accountability in the racialized past and its present manifestations. This narrative of reconciliation gives pride of place to the toxic, shared mythology of race, where it remains in attitudes, in coded speech, in theatrics of protest, in policy, in fact. The Right has been astoundingly effective at pushing the boundaries of toleration, as was the Confederacy, searching for political victory, a totalitarian state once and for all, and not simply one for people of color, a bonfire fueled by all the oil in the world to cauterize what can only be described as a hole in the bottom of their spirit.

In the post–civil rights world a system of symbols has replaced the hard work of true integration. By testifying to the conditions of African Americans in racial terms and listening to these testimonies in racial terms we feel open-minded and individually absolved whenever we "learn something" that has been around our entire lives. It is a ritual enactment of pain and catharsis. None of this provides absolution, let alone atonement, yet it blinds us to the real goal, stealing purpose from the march toward full integration, which is still further away and more demanding than we wish. If we do not reframe the problem and re-devote ourselves, the only certainty is we will never reach our goal, which is as Richard Nixon and George Wallace wished.

As I write this, the United States Supreme Court has just handed down a ruling making it easier for the state of Ohio to strike voters from the rolls, for Florida to institute a de facto poll tax, for Republican legislatures to create electoral maps that defy the will of the people. It is, we are asked to believe, only coincidental that those most likely to be stricken are from poor and minority communities. Donald Trump was not impeached as he would have been in a truly civil society, even as his corruption and boldness grow day by day. He has made clear he does not serve the United States, but the old gods of whiteness. Suppression of the black vote has been an integral strategy of white supremacy since the colonial era. Stripping blacks of the right to vote was one of the very first bricks in the institution of slavery and one of the very first ways the progress of Reconstruction was clawed back. The American right wing and its bedfellows still do not want this to be a democracy.

There have been so many attacks on the progress of the sixties that we have gone from alarm to silent acceptance when a
little more is chiseled away. Integration, of course, might seem
like an abstraction when democracy itself feels under attack, but
race has always been the chisel.

In the current moment, the omnipresence of cameras has
made many newly aware of the police brutality that has been
present in a nation that has always viewed blacks as a threat special enough to suspend civil liberties. Despite the theater of outrage, there has been no systemic change.

In the present moment, school segregation is a national crisis or would be in a country committed to an educated citizenry.
In the current moment, wealth inequalities have surpassed levels
seen during the great robber baron years of the early twentieth
century, when the rights of labor were violently suppressed and a
small number of the wealthiest not only discovered that American politicians could be bought, and public opinion manipulated, but they actively corrupted both. In the present moment,
America has the most advanced, costly health-care complex in
the world, but its black infants have more than twice the mor-
tality rate of white infants, those citizens who do survive live
shorter lives plagued by deadly diseases caused by environmental
stress, and health-care practitioners provide them less thorough
treatment. In the present moment, the problems persist from
the cradle to the grave. The United States is the only Western
democracy in the world that sanctions the death penalty in its
penal code.

In the current climate the president of the United States
draws renewed support every time he asserts that immigrants
(read Central Americans of indigenous descent) are driving

up the crime rate, when he attacks black football players for protesting against injustice in society, when he calls African countries "shitholes." There is a part of the population that, naturally given our history, applauds the offense because it reinforces the myth of whiteness. But just as crucially, by going on the attack, it forces everyone else into the reactive position of protesting insults instead of the real crimes being committed. We feel in our protest of such offenses a confirmation that we are acting, when in fact we are ceding our own agency instead of maintaining focus on truer goals of equality.

The fact that the country could move so easily to authoritarian declarations of racism proves not merely how close to the surface they are but also that this is the other pole of the nation. It is not a difference in fiscal policy or foreign policy but between democracy and white supremacy that constitutes the base of the current Republican Party, which to those within the party is more important than the country. This was a core fear of the founding generation, that self-interested political parties could defeat the revolution from the inside. The real question is how willing we are to tolerate it. How long?

Twentieth-century attempts at what was called racial healing and tolerance began in the premise that we must learn new ways of seeing, accepting, and putting up with one another. We learned a great deal from these efforts, especially those of us who have had direct experience from a young age, and there is every reason to continue them: after all, the *effects* of race remain all too real.

Yet one might better argue that what is necessary is a fundamental *unlearning* of the false things the past five hundred years have inculcated in modern society. Without unlearning, the received falseness will always be present, and all our words and deeds are dodges. Only integration can achieve a goal so lofty because only integration removes the prerequisites for a racially determined society, along with its cries of credulity and remorse every time something happens in this country that runs counter to the ways we wish to be seen and the things we wish to believe; only integration refuses to pay the poll tax of the past or accept the daily reports of social death and political murder.

Integration scythes through the fig leaf of language to abolish at root that which blinds us most, including our attempts to "understand" race, as though race made any sense and was worth understanding. So what if we recite, like a catechism, the fact that race touches all our institutions and all of us individually even in ways we do not suspect? So what if we claim to know that our society has been organized around such falseness since the seventeenth century? So what if we have done so many "studies" of race that we know its atomic weight, its different states, its variants? So what if we now know all there is to know about race?

Why shouldn't we? After all, we invented it. We re-create it every day. But we still suffer an appalling failure of will when it comes to the real goal of the civil rights movement, which began before the Civil War: always, and rightfully, integration.

Race can morph and hide. Subjected to any scrutiny, it demands to morph and hide, claiming to be color-blind, claiming to be woke, reinforcing itself by demanding absolutely nothing that affects the core of the problem. The core of the problem is the fear of and flight from integration. The race line is comforting; what lies beyond the race line is what scares the hell out of America because it is so unknown, and not only in America. It plagues every country on every continent where the pestilence of slavery and colonialism was allowed to spread: in Europe, in South America, in the Caribbean, in South Africa. This is the goal that remains under attack because what it means, for anyone firmly committed to the abolition of oppression, is the full acceptance of regular black and brown people into the opportunities of American life. The same deal as everyone else, and not feigned helplessness or the theater of false awakening when we encounter the problems first encountered during the revolutionary generation. This, as James Baldwin said sixty years ago, "is not a southern problem. It is a national problem. What is happening in New Orleans today began to happen over a hundred years ago when in effect the North, the government, began to free tens of thousands of individuals who were black. They made no provision for them. None whatever. None whatever. None whatever. They were stumped."[4] Are we still stumped?

In the three generations since Baldwin's statement, one of the things we have learned is how capable race is of adapting across historical eras, accommodating itself to supposedly neutral innovations in science, technology, media, culture, and on into the modern age of global humanity. It is a disease equipped with an evolutionary machinery to protect itself. When we privilege race, we remain in the field of whiteness that binds together an immoral compromise between North and South, liberal and conservative, English and Spanish, people otherwise at war but agreed on the need for cheap labor and a cheap ego hit that tells not who you are but who you are not. Identity by negation, a bankrupt mythology of self that warps democracies all around the world, taking as they do the United States for their model.

To know what is on the other side of a chasm, one first has to cross it. Even in most of America's most liberal institutions and public spaces, what passes for crossing this chasm is in reality a surface representation, seldom a fully normal, mutually accountable interaction among equals. Integration means not only equal opportunity, and mutual ability to empathize across social paradigms, but ultimately the equal ability to shape one's life, society, and future as a full participant in every sphere of American life. For the moment we have settled for the tacit understanding that by allowing some, we are collectively freed from the complex problems of the many.

To break free of this is to follow democracy to its natural conclusion, but it means letting go of the old pagan gods of hatred; secret, unearned advantage; and private vanities to submit to an equal society, which is what democracy promises but something this human world has never seen because it takes away the comfort of false pride from you as well as from me.

Lasting progress has been achieved only through the heroic action of the many who wish to move beyond the past and the impasse we find ourselves at again and again, with each generation making peace with the same compromise or the idea that more cannot be done.

Much more can be done. However, it is an active process, as opposed to the reactive forces by which we have come to the present conversation, in which one accepts an untenable situation in exchange for material and psychological comfort, until the society begins to fail you as it failed those before, again and again and again for the simple reason that it has never been supportable.

Integration, like the Civil War, like the civil rights movement, deals in cold facts and forces on each (individual, institution, organization) the responsibility of what to do with them. At least until it has become the new myth and norm.

There are traumas in the historical past that may be impossible to heal. Wrongs absolute, but formative. The only balm for wrongs in the past is present behavior and the future one creates. Integration is *the* American problem to address if for no other reason than America is the first and oldest democracy, and success or failure here presages the fate of democracy in the world.

No other generation in America has been as equipped to address this question as the current ones because no previous generation has been as produced by the *possibility* of integration. The things that were theory fifty years ago are now the lives we live and lead and battle with and aspire to. At least some of us. Nor will any bear so much blame if we allow ourselves to be turned back into the past or settle for half-steps: what we have witnessed so far affirms the theory that it is a better way to live and the right way to be.

It is morning of the first day after the Civil War.

The questions come like nature itself: What did you dream? What do you wish? How will you achieve it? Will you reunite the Union as it was before, living among the dead until you are also a ghost, or bury the past and build a new city atop the Rome that once was?

That is what I ask myself certain mornings after I read the news or have an unpleasant encounter with a stranger or someone I partially know. When I am beleaguered for reasons that deal less with my own foibles and make no other sense, or else try to explain again things that are clear and settled, which too many claim not to see. The spirit of some New England slave captain hiding in terror belowdecks, under the eyelids of a passerby or familiar, until the revolt is over. The caterwauling of two Ibo children being kidnapped while playing in their front yard. Some poor Confederate riding the subway in purgatory, in a restaurant, on television, who does not yet know the war is over, that he died long ago. It is only ghosts, I say. I find it helps, and so you may wish to tell yourself, too.

It is morning of the first day after the Civil War, and I wear the Pacific blue of the Union Army, which I wish only to consign to the attic. Old Abe Lincoln is in Washington turning gray as presidents do. My friends and relatives and enemies on the other side of an unbridgeable divide dressed in the gray doom of the Atlantic will, someday soon, at last repent. I hold no grudge but memories of my own, of what we fought for, as I write a final letter home, knowing well it may not reach its destination. It is only a few paltry lines. They will repent, and their leaders will too. There will be peace and the new nation I once heard foretold. I walk with daily devotion home now to make love and children and plow my own fields and not think of any of this again. It is the first morning on the first day after the Civil War. I will be home again soon.

What remains to ask is not whether our goals are attainable. We have seen they are. The question is simply the test given to the American people from the founding era to our own: How much of the revolutionary spirit of this thing we call democracy do you still have in you?

ACKNOWLEDGMENTS

When I was a sophomore or junior in high school, the late J. Z. Smith, a renowned historian of religion, lecturer, and dean at the University of Chicago, whose home I was visiting one day, happened to peer into the assigned textbook for my AP history class. He chuckled to himself, then peered at me and laughed out loud. He suggested that I instead read an essay by a long-ago philosopher and come see him again to report my thoughts. Reading the essay, which I later learned was notoriously difficult, felt like landing on a strange shore on a moonless night. I couldn't make much sense of it at all.

I don't remember what rambling answer I must have given when I next saw him. He simply told me to go read it again. Then a third time. It was a great boon when I returned after that, and we began to read it together. I imagine some sort of sense must have gotten into me about the mind-spirit, scientific knowledge, the history of ideas, and narratives of culture and history. I certainly didn't distinguish myself in any way, but I learned a great deal about reading, eventually teaching, generosity, and humility. He was a mighty signal from an ancient source, and is still, as he might say, transmitting.

Among the hundreds of sources I consulted over the course of this book, those of David Blight at Yale, Randal Kennedy at Harvard, and David Nasaw at the Graduate Center made a strong enough impression on me, and I believe contemporary scholarship in general, to merit additional acknowledgment. They are not only great thinkers, but original ones as well.

Richard Deming, Michael Cunningham, and Caryl Phillips (whose rightful acknowledgment deserves more than this line) gave me the opportunity to teach at Yale and get to know the community of writers and thinkers there. More personally they provided a welcome sense of friendship and belonging, as did the students in my English 365 class. If I do not name you individually it is because I want the world to hear from you directly, which it will and soon.

Stacy and Charles D. King and Staci R. Collins Jackson at Macro provided me uncommon access to Hollywood, allowing me to see it in a new light. Lucy Crawford at TEDMED and Michael Painter at the Robert Wood Johnson Foundation helped me better understand the intersection of medicine and society. Clive Priddle, Jaime Leifer, Lindsay Fradkoff, Johanna Dickson, and Melissa Veronesi at Bold Type Books took the leap of faith that made this work possible and gave it the best kind of support.

My conversations with Linda Holliday and Ali Naqvi, Maximillian Coreth and Marine Hartogs, Richard Abate, Tanya McKinnon, Chris Jackson, Tracy Sherrod, Abe Hsuan, Lilly Farahnakian and David Silverman, Rich Ma, Lee Maicon, Ed Castillo, Jia Jia, Ian Mount and Cintra Scott, Ghenete Wright Muir, Vicki Skovle, Margaret Litvin, Nora Lewontin-Rojas, Ariane Fink, Francisco Goldman, Alejandro Zamba, and Jon Lee Anderson reminded me of where this conversation began. They renewed my faith, again and again, in where it is meant to go.

Sarah Chalfant and Rebecca Nagel at The Wylie Agency have superpowers, including telekinesis, invisibility, and telepathy. Most wondrous of all—humanity.

Katy O'Donnell, my editor, selflessly helped make this a most joyful labor. She deserves more praise than can be told, and so I sing it.

NOTES

Preface

1. Quoted in Nancy Stepan, "Race and the Return of the Great Chain of Being, 1800–50," in *The Idea of Race in Science: Great Britain 1800–1960* (London: Palgrave Macmillan, 1982).

2. "Massive Resistance," Virginia Museum of History & Culture, www .virginiahistory.org/collections-and-resources/virginia-history-explorer/civil -rights-movement-virginia/massive.

Introduction: The Lie of Demographics

1. Immanuel Kant, in one of the foundational texts of democracy, *A General Theory of History*, describes this distinction as an essential difference between the public and private spheres. An incredible amount hinges on how these are shaped and defined, and where the power to do so resides.

2. With modern remnants in overseas protectorates such as Puerto Rico and the Philippines.

Chapter 1: When We Were English

1. *This Day in History,* History Channel, August 20, 2019, www.history .com/this-day-in-history/first-african-slave-ship-arrives-jamestown-colony.

2. Brendan Wolfe, "Free Blacks in Colonial Virginia," *Encyclopedia Virginia*, Virginia Humanities, May 13, 2019, www.encyclopediavirginia.org /Free_Blacks_in_Colonial_Virginia.

3. Quoted in Thomas J. Davis, *History of African Americans: Exploring Diverse Roots* (Santa Barbara, CA: Greenwood, 2016), 21.

4. Alexis de Tocqueville, *Democracy in America*, trans. Henry Reeve (Boston: John Allyn, 1876), 1:457.

5. "The Middle Passage," National Park Service, March 10, 2017, www .nps.gov/articles/the-middle-passage.htm.

6. William Shakespeare, *Othello*, The Complete Works of William Shakespeare, http://shakespeare.mit.edu/index.html.

7. Shakespeare, *Othello*.

8. One might also read him as a most mischievous symbol of democracy, in which free will opens a Pandora's box of mischief and unruliness itself is part of human nature.

9. Shakespeare, *Othello*.

10. He also lives by the sword in a play in which all the soldiers are doomed.

11. Ernest Hemingway, *A Farewell to Arms* (New York: Scribner, 1929), 271.

Chapter 2: The Toll of Independence

1. "Thomas Jefferson and Sally Hemings: A Brief Account," Thomas Jefferson Foundation, www.monticello.org/thomas-jefferson/jefferson-slavery /thomas-jefferson-and-sally-hemings-a-brief-account.

2. Unlike her counterparts in European courts, most of them polygamous for all practical purposes, where the king's concubine was a very, high -status position.

3. Quoted in Richard E. Dickson, "Jefferson and Slavery," Thomas Jefferson Heritage Society, www.tjheritage.org/jefferson-and-slavery.

4. Quoted in Stephen K. McDowell, *Building Godly Nations: Lessons from the Bible and America's Christian History* (Charlottesville, VA: Providence Foundation, 2004), 220–221.

5. John Quincy Adams, "The Crime of Slavery," speech at Newburyport, July 4, 1837, Bartleby.com, www.bartleby.com/400/prose/691.html.

6. Quoted in Paris Amanda Spies-Gans, "James Madison," Princeton & Slavery, https://slavery.princeton.edu/stories/james-madison.

7. "Slave, Free Black, and White Population, 1780–1830," https:// userpages.umbc.edu/~bouton/History407/SlaveStats.htm.

8. Winthrop D. Jordan, *White over Black: American Attitudes Toward the Negro, 1550–1812*, 2nd ed. (Chapel Hill: University of North Carolina Press, 2012), 310.

9. Quoted in "The Mere Distinction of Colour," James Madison's Montpelier, www.montpelier.org/visit/mere-distinction.

10. John Quincy Adams, "Argument Before the Supreme Court," February 24 and March 1, 1841, Yale University, Gilder Lehrman Center for the Study of Slavery, Resistance, and Abolition, https://glc.yale.edu /argument-john-quincy-adams-supreme-court.

11. de Tocqueville, *Democracy in America*, 1:339.

12. de Tocqueville, *Democracy in America*, 1:337.

13. John Sullivan, "Education of Negro Children," in *Children & Youth in America: A Documentary History*, vol. 1, *1600–1865*, ed. Robert H. Bremner (Cambridge, MA: Harvard University Press, 1970), 337.

14. de Tocqueville, *Democracy in America*, 1:424, 1:445.

15. de Tocqueville, *Democracy in America*, 1:187.

Chapter 3: Forgetting and Remembrance

1. It is no coincidence the market where Africans and Native Americans were traded in New York City was at the river end of Wall Street.

2. Milton Crowe, interview by Calvin Baker, 1999.

3. Olaudah Equiano, *The Interesting Narrative of the Life of Olaudah Equiano, or Gustavus Vassa, the African—Written by Himself, Printed for and Sold by the Author* (London, 1789).

4. "Slavery in America," Battle of Franklin Trust, https://boft.org/slavery-in-america.

5. Janet Sharp Hermann, *Joseph E. Davis: Pioneer Patriarch* (Jackson: University Press of Mississippi, 2007).

6. Hermann, *Joseph E. Davis*.

7. It happens that Lord Murray was guardian to his black niece, Dido Elizabeth Belle, who had been born a slave when her father, Sir John Lindsay, was an admiral of the Royal Navy stationed in the West Indies. After Olaudah Equiano bought his freedom, the Philadelphia merchant who owned his contract offered him a partnership in his trading company. Fearing that his only fate anywhere in the Americas was to be captured and sold again, he moved to London and set up shop on his own in Marylebone.

8. Of course it also reports on attitudes of the time, as well as the reparations argument, to note that when slavery was ended across the empire, restitution was made to former slave owners but not former slaves.

9. Quoted in David W. Blight, *Frederick Douglass: Prophet of Freedom* (New York: Simon & Schuster, 2018).

10. David W. Blight, *Race and Reunion* (Cambridge, MA: Harvard University Press, 2009), 13.

11. Blight, *Race and Reunion*.

12. Quoted in Waldo E. Martin Jr., *The Mind of Frederick Douglass* (Chapel Hill: University of North Carolina Press, 2000), 65.

13. Frederick Douglass, *The Speeches of Frederick Douglass: A Critical Edition*, ed. John R. McKivigan, Julie Husband, and Heather L. Kaufman (New Haven, CT: Yale University Press, 2018), 251.

14. Frederick Douglass, *The Life of Frederick Douglass: Complete Autobiographies, Speeches & Personal Letters in One Volume* (Madison & Adams Press, 2018).

15. Melissa Block, "Here's What's Become of a Historic All-Black Town in the Mississippi Delta," NPR, March 8, 2017, www.npr.org /2017/03/08/515814287/heres-whats-become-of-a-historic-all-black-town -in-the-mississippi-delta.

16. Quoted in Janet Sharp Hermann, *The Pursuit of a Dream* (Jackson: University of Mississippi Press, 1999).

Chapter 4: The Land Without Memory

1. Frederick Douglass, "The Color Line in America," *North American Review* 132 (1881).

2. Douglass, *The Life of Frederick Douglass.*

3. Quoted in Randy E. Barnett and Josh Blackman, *Constitutional Rights: Cases in Context*, 2nd ed. (New York: Wolters Kluwer, 2018).

4. Blight, *Frederick Douglass.*

5. Joellyn Zollman, "Jewish Immigration to America: Three Waves," My Jewish Learning, www.myjewishlearning.com/article/jewish-immi gration-to-america-three-waves.

6. Ira Katznelson, *When Affirmative Action Was White* (New York: W. W. Norton, 2006).

7. David Nasaw, *Going Out: The Rise and Fall of Public Amusements* (Cambridge, MA: Harvard University Press, 1999), 47–48.

8. Both projection and admission that the world needed to be saved from those who behaved as you did.

Chapter 5: American Empire: From Periphery to Center

1. "Beyond HOLC," T-Races, http://salt.umd.edu/T-RACES/holc .html.

2. Walter F. Mondale, "Walter Mondale: The Civil Rights Law We Ignored," *New York Times*, April 10, 2018, www.nytimes.com/2018/04/10 /opinion/walter-mondale-fair-housing-act.html.

3. David A. Graham, Adrienne Green, Cullen Murphy, and Parker Richards, "An Oral History of Trump's Racism," *Atlantic*, June 2019, www .theatlantic.com/magazine/archive/2019/06/trump-racism-comments /588067.

4. There was not a northern liberal in the highest office in the forty-five years between Kennedy and Obama. The Left has been appeasing the

Right since the Constitutional Convention. Even the Civil War was about defense. The simple mathematical reason is that white liberals have never been as reliably committed to equal rights as white conservatives are to racism.

5. And, historically, at least an interracial endeavor.

6. "African Americans and the New Deal," Digital History, www .digitalhistory.uh.edu/disp_textbook.cfm?smtID=2&psid=3447.

7. The story in agriculture was particularly grim. Although 40 percent of all black workers made their living as sharecroppers and tenant farmers, Agricultural Adjustment Administration (AAA) policies intended to protect white landowners would force 100,000 into unemployment in 1933 and 1934.

8. "African Americans and the New Deal."

9. Quoted in Charles M. Blow, "Race, to the Finish," *New York Times*, November 12, 2014, www.nytimes.com/2014/11/13/opinion/charles-blow -race-to-the-finish.html.

10. The Nazis were also avid students of US segregation.

11. "Executive Order 8802," EEOC, June 25, 1941, www.eeoc.gov /eeoc/history/35th/thelaw/eo-8802.html.

12. Quoted in Nick Kotz, "'When Affirmative Action Was White': Uncivil Rights," *New York Times*, August 28, 2005, www.nytimes.com/2005 /08/28/books/review/when-affirmative-action-was-white-uncivil-rights .html.

13. Katznelson, *When Affirmative Action Was White.*

14. David A. Bateman, Ira Katznelson, and John S. Lapinski, "How Southern Politicians Defended White Supremacy—and Made the South Poorer," *Washington Post*, November 26, 2018, www.washingtonpost.com /news/monkey-cage/wp/2018/11/26/how-southern-politicians-defended -white-supremacy-and-made-the-south-poorer.

15. Brandon Weber, "How African American WWII Veterans Were Scorned by the G.I. Bill," *Progressive*, November 10, 2017, https://progressive .org/dispatches/how-african-american-wwii-veterans-were-scorned-by-the -g-i-b.

16. Weber, "How African American WWII Veterans Were Scorned by the G.I. Bill."

17. Weber, "How African American WWII Veterans Were Scorned by the G.I. Bill."

18. Karen E. Fields and Barbara J. Fields, *Racecraft: The Soul of Inequality in American Life* (London: Verso, 2014).

Chapter 6: The Death of the Civil Rights Movement

1. The Left was first replaced by the "New Left" and subsequently by a "third wave," each iteration progressively more institutional and materialist than its predecessor.

2. Stokely Carmichael and Charles V. Hamilton, *Black Power: The Politics of Liberation* (New York: Random House, 1967).

3. Robin DiAngelo, *White Fragility: Why It's So Hard for White People to Talk About Racism* (Boston: Beacon, 2018).

4. Robin DiAngelo, "White Fragility," *International Journal of Critical Pedagogy* 3 (2011): 54–64, http://libjournal.uncg.edu/index.php/ijcp/article /view/249.

5. "The FBI Sets Goals for COINTELPRO," Herb: Social History for Every Classroom, American Social History Project, https://herb.ashp.cuny .edu/items/show/814.

6. "October 1966 Black Panther Party Platform and Program," The Sixties Project, www2.iath.virginia.edu/sixties/HTML_docs/Resources /Primary/Manifestos/Panther_platform.html.

Chapter 7: Affirmative Action, Diversity, and Symbolism

1. Gavin Evans, *Skin Deep: Journeys in the Divisive Science of Race* (London: OneWorld, 2019).

2. There is a cascading problem when public universities are not held in the same regard or funded at the same level. There are equally smart people across this country and many things to critique about the Ivy League. What is really being fought over is not education but status with the undemocratic logic that access to a small handful of high schools leads to a small handful of universities, which leads in turn to a handful of networks and corporations that control the nation's wealth. Class mobility in the US is among the lowest in developed nations. According to the National Bureau of Economic Research, of the factors that determine upward mobility in the US, "The first is segregation: areas that are more residentially segregated by race and income have lower levels of mobility." The other major factors include race—for example, there is less mobility for blacks than for whites—and the K–12 school system. See www.nber.org/papers/w19843.

3. When I say "black" in the rest of this book, I mean it literally but also metaphorically as a stand-in for all people of color. The specifics of otherization and terms of assimilation differ, but the overarching mechanism described in the previous chapter is the same. When we speak of model minorities, we may as well substitute the antebellum terms "good negro" and "bad negro." I do not say this lightly or to give offense but to point out the

difference in terms of acceptance. Certainly one can imagine a buffer class of Asians or recent Nigerian immigrants (the most academically creden-tialed people in the country). The function is ever the same. A citizen is a citizen.

4. Eliza Shapiro, "Only 7 Black Students Got into Stuyvesant, N.Y.'s Most Selective High School, Out of 895 Spots," *New York Times*, March 18, 2019, www.nytimes.com/2019/03/18/nyregion/black-students-nyc-high -schools.html.

5. Reema Amin, "As New York City Starts Collecting Data on In-equalities in PTA Fundraising, the Search Is on for Potential Solutions," Chalkbeat, November 2, 2018, www.chalkbeat.org/posts/ny/2018/11/02 /as-city-starts-collecting-data-on-inequities-in-pta-fundraising-the-search -is-on-for-potential-solutions.

6. OECD, "A Family Affair: Intergenerational Social Mobility Across OECD Countries," in *Economic Policy Reforms 2010: Going for Growth* (Paris: OECD Publishing, 2010), https://doi.org/10.1787/growth-2010-38-en.

7. Quoted in Valerie Strauss, "Why School Integration Works," *Wash-ington Post*, May 16, 2019, www.washingtonpost.com/education/2019/05/16 /why-school-integration-works.

8. Alvin Chang, "The Data Proves That School Segregation Is Get-ting Worse," Vox, March 5, 2018, www.vox.com/2018/3/5/17080218 /school-segregation-getting-worse-data.

9. Richard Rothstein, "The Racial Achievement Gap, Segre-gated Schools, and Segregated Neighborhoods—A Constitutional In-sult," Economic Policy Institute, November 12, 2014, www.epi.org /publication/the-racial-achievement-gap-segregated-schools-and-segregated -neighborhoods-a-constitutional-insult.

10. Erica Frankenburg, Jongyeon Ee, Jennifer B. Ayscue, and Gary Orfield, "Harming Our Common Future: America's Segregated Schools 65 Years After *Brown*," Civil Rights Project, Center for Education and Civil Rights, May 10, 2019, www.civilrightsproject.ucla.edu/research/k-12 -education/integration-and-diversity/harming-our-common-future -americas-segregated-schools-65-years-after-brown/Brown-65-050919v4 -final.pdf.

11. Valerie Strauss, "Is It Finally Time to Get Rid of the SAT and ACT College Admissions Tests?" *Washington Post*, March 19, 2019, www .washingtonpost.com/education/2019/03/19/is-it-finally-time-get-rid-sat -act-college-admissions-tests.

12. Diversity is not a rubric in rankings criteria. Rejection rates are. In-stead of dancing to the fiddle of rankings I do not understand why the "best"

schools don't simply opt out or at least make the rankings reflect what the schools value. It would be healthier for the whole country.

13. Is it too much to suggest he's a Jewish man in the South performing whiteness in the same way Clarence Thomas has made himself one of the most conservative members of the American bench, from a sense of social insecurity, intelligence, and unfathomable rage at the world?

14. Even if one stripped all the cultural influences from test results, the margin of error for each section is 60 points, or approximately four percentiles. There is not only no statistical difference between the 25th and 75th percentile at Harvard; there is no statistical difference between the top 30 universities, or top 17 liberal arts schools, or between the "best" liberal arts school and the "best" big school. The 23rd-ranked liberal arts school, Harvey Mudd, has a higher average SAT than Stanford. Of these top 50 schools, only 10 percent are public institutions. Couple this with the impact of test prep, and within fairly wide statistical bands the tests aren't telling you a whole lot, nor are rankings, except our own socioeconomic anxieties and social destruction. Given the way that they have been manipulated and natural fluctuations, the tests don't have great meaning within five percentiles, and grade definition varies even more. After a certain threshold you can take whomever you want. At the extreme end of the curve these two data points tell you about as much as a driving test. Taken at face value, 20,000 people will be in the first percentile every year, more students than there are spots in the Ivy League. Across the statistical band that's 80,000 students. These were never meant to be the only credentials that mattered in America. It's a form of rent-seeking by the testing companies and list makers. Calculated using data from various sources.

15. "Fast Facts: Back to School Statistics," National Center for Educational Statistics, https://nces.ed.gov/fastfacts/display.asp?id=372.

16. The national poverty average is 11.8 percent. It is 24.5 percent for Native Americans, 20.8 percent for African Americans, 18 percent for Latinx households, and 12.3 percent for Asian Americans. This means that about 316,000 poor white kids, 114,450 poor black kids, 108,000 poor Latinx kids, 26,000 poor Asian American kids, and 19,000 poor Native American kids graduate from high school every year. Calculated using data from USCensus .gov.

Chapter 8: The Mainstreaming of Black Music

1. Frederick Douglass, *Narrative of the Life of Frederick Douglass: An American Slave* (New York: Cosimo Classics, 2008).

2. "The Beastie Boys," Encyclopedia.com, November 2, 2019, www
.encyclopedia.com/education/news-wires-white-papers-and-books/beastie
-boys.

Chapter 9: Pastime

1. Quoted in "William George Beers," Wikipedia, September 19, 2019,
https://en.wikipedia.org/wiki/William_George_Beers.

2. Dan Gartland, "Jim Brown May Have Been Even Better at Lacrosse
Than He Was at Football," *Sports Illustrated*, February 17, 2016, www.si.com
/nfl/jim-brown-nfl-hall-fame-syracuse-lacrosse.

3. George Vecsey, "Jim Brown's Best Sport," *New York Times*, March
19, 1984, www.nytimes.com/1984/03/19/sports/jim-brown-s-best-sport
.html.

4. Ryan Cortes, "Jim Brown Retires on the Set of 'The Dirty Dozen,'"
The Undefeated, July 13, 2016, https://theundefeated.com/features/jim
-brown-retires-while-on-the-set-of-the-dirty-dozen.

5. Tim Layden, "Why Jim Brown Matters," *Sports Illustrated*, October 6, 2015, www.si.com/nfl/2015/10/06/jim-brown-cleveland-browns
-hall-of-fame-nfl-greatness.

6. Quoted in Gary Myers, *How 'Bout Them Cowboys? Inside the Hud-
dle with the Stars and Legends of America's Team* (New York: Grand Central,
2018).

7. Quoted in John Wagner and Mark Maske, "Trump: NFL Players Unwilling to Stand for Anthem Maybe 'Shouldn't Be in the Country,'"
Washington Post, May 24, 2018, www.washingtonpost.com/politics/trump
-nfl-owners-doing-the-right-thing-on-national-anthem-policy/2018/05/24
/cdd66490-5f36-11e8-a4a4-c070ef53f315_story.html.

8. Andrew Lawrence, "The NFL Is 70% Black, So Why Is Its TV
Coverage So White?" *Guardian*, January 31, 2019, www.theguardian.com
/sport/2019/jan/31/nfl-tv-coverage-racial-demographics-super-bowl.

9. Karen Grigsby Bates, "When It Comes to Race and Sports, Who
Owns an Athlete's Opinions?" NPR, October 21, 2017, www.npr.org
/sections/codeswitch/2017/10/21/557692016/when-it-comes-to-race
-and-sports-who-owns-an-athletes-opinions.

10. Lawrence, "The NFL Is 70% Black, So Why Is Its TV Coverage So
White?"

11. He inherited the team, but when it comes to extremes of wealth, an
exception to the general rule of rents, new money always has more than old
money.

12. Quoted in George Solomon, "'Jimmy the Greek' Fired by CBS for His Remarks," *Washington Post*, January 17, 1988, www.washingtonpost .com/archive/politics/1988/01/17/jimmy-the-greek-fired-by-cbs-for-his -remarks/27536e46-3031-40c2-bb2b-f912ec518f80.

13. E. Franklin Frazier, *The Negro Family in the United States* (Chicago: University of Chicago Press, 1939).

14. "Chris Rock: Never Scared (2004)—Full Transcript," Notes from the Loft, January 19, 2018, https://scrapsfromtheloft.com/2018/01/19 /chris-rock-never-scared-2004-full-transcript.

15. "LeBron James Says NFL Team Owners Have 'Slave Mentality,'" *Guardian*, December 22, 2018, www.theguardian.com/sport/2018/dec/22 /lebron-james-nfl-team-owners-have-slave-mentality.

16. "LeBron James Says NFL Team Owners Have 'Slave Mentality.'"

Chapter 10: Hipsters in the City

1. "Social Experience Drives Empathetic, Pro-social Behavior in Rats," UChicagoMedicine, January 14, 2014, www.uchicagomedicine .org/forefront/news/2014/january/social-experience-drives-empathetic -pro-social-behavior-in-rats.

2. Evans, *Skin Deep*.

3. Quoted in Troy Parks, "How Racism, Segregation Drive Health Dis- parities," American Medical Association, December 15, 2016, www.ama-assn .org/delivering-care/patient-support-advocacy/how-racism-segregation -drive-health-disparities.

4. Quoted in Parks, "How Racism, Segregation Drive Health Disparities."

5. David R. Williams, "How Racism Makes Us Sick," TEDMED, No- vember 2016, www.ted.com/talks/david_r_williams_how_racism_makes _us_sick.

6. Williams, "How Racism Makes Us Sick."

7. Sullivan, "Education of Negro Children," 337.

8. John R. Logan, ed., *Diversity and Disparities: America Enters a New Century* (New York: Russell Sage Foundation, 2014).

9. Race warps the behaviors that Marx predicted from the time black indenture became slavery, continuing through political, economic, and me- dia formulations like the "white working class," the offshoring of production (largely to women in the developing world), and the opacity of political infor- mation on a global scale. Martin Luther King noted this warp when his focus shifted from race as a stand-alone phenomenon to his three-point strategy of race, poverty, and militarism.

10. Kevin M. Kruse, *White Flight: Atlanta and the Making of Modern Conservatism* (Princeton, NJ: Princeton University Press, 2007).

11. "Haldeman Diary Shows Nixon Was Wary of Blacks and Jews," *New York Times*, May 18, 1994, www.nytimes.com/1994/05/18/us/haldeman -diary-shows-nixon-was-wary-of-blacks-and-jews.html.

12. During the 1988 presidential election, the Willie Horton attack ads run against Democratic candidate Michael Dukakis built upon the "Southern Strategy" in a campaign that reinforced the notion that Republicans best represent conservative whites with traditional values. Lee Atwater and Roger Ailes worked on the campaign as George H. W. Bush's political strategists. Upon seeing a favorable New Jersey focus group response to the Horton strategy, Atwater recognized that an implicit racial appeal could work outside of the southern states. The subsequent ads featured Horton's mug shot and played on fears of black criminals. As Atwater said of the strategy, "By the time we're finished, they're going to wonder whether Willie Horton is Dukakis' running mate." Al Gore was the first to use the Willie Horton prison furlough against Dukakis and—like the Bush campaign—would not mention race. The Bush campaign claimed it was initially made aware of the Horton issue via the Gore campaign's use of the subject. Bush initially hesitated to use the Horton campaign strategy, but the campaign saw it as a wedge issue to harm Dukakis, who was struggling against Democratic rival Jesse Jackson. See Rick Perlstein, "Exclusive: Lee Atwater's Infamous 1981 Interview on the Southern Strategy," *Nation*, November 13, 2012, www.thenation.com /article/exclusive-lee-atwaters-infamous-1981-interview-southern-strategy.

In addition to presidential campaigns, subsequent Republican campaigns for the House of Representatives and Senate employed the Southern Strategy. During his 1990 reelection campaign, Jesse Helms attacked his opponent's alleged support of "racial quotas," most notably through an ad in which a white person's hands are seen crumpling a letter indicating that he was denied a job because of the color of his skin.

As *New York Times* opinion columnist Bob Herbert wrote in 2005, "The truth is that there was very little that was subconscious about the G.O.P.'s relentless appeal to racist whites. Tired of losing elections, it saw an opportunity to renew itself by opening its arms wide to white voters who could never forgive the Democratic Party for its support of civil rights and voting rights for blacks." Aistrup described the transition of the Southern Strategy, saying that it has "evolved from a states' rights, racially conservative message to one promoting in the Nixon years, vis-à-vis the courts, a racially conservative interpretation of civil rights laws—including opposition to busing. With the ascendancy of Reagan, the Southern Strategy became a national strategy that melded race, taxes, anticommunism, and religion." See Joseph A. Aistrup, *The Southern Strategy Revisited: Republican Top-Down Advancement in the South* (Lexington: University of Kentucky Press, 1996).

13. Alvin Chang, quoted in Terrell Carter, *Healing Racial Divides: Finding Strength in Our Diversity* (St. Louis, MO: Chalice Press, 2019).

14. University of Southern California, "Gentrification Draws More Whites to Minority Neighborhoods," Phys.org, May 1, 2018, https://phys.org/news/2018-05-gentrification-whites-minority-neighborhoods.html.

15. Andrew Small, "The Gentrification of Gotham," City Lab, April 28, 2017, www.citylab.com/life/2017/04/the-gentrification-of-gotham/524694.

16. James Baldwin, *The Price of the Ticket: Collected Nonfiction, 1948–1985* (New York: Macmillan, 1985), 466–467.

17. Abigail Thernstrom and Stephan Thernstrom, "Black Progress: How Far We've Come, and How Far We Have to Go," Brookings, March 1, 1998, www.brookings.edu/articles/black-progress-how-far-weve-come-and-how-far-we-have-to-go.

18. "Affirmative Action: Primary Beneficiaries Are White Women," NileValleyPeoples, April 8, 2011, http://nilevalleypeoples.blogspot.com/2011/04/affirmative-action-primary.html.

Chapter 11: This Is Us? Ambivalence and Representation

1. References only refer to season 1; Kevin does date a black woman in a later season.

2. Mark Voger, "David Chase on Rock 'n' Roll, 'Casual Racism' and Offbeat Endings," Advance Local, March 30, 2019, www.nj.com/entertainment/2013/04/david_chase_not_fade_away.html.

3. Edward W. Said, *Culture and Imperialism* (New York: Knopf, 1993).

Part III: In Light of the *White Lion*

1. de Tocqueville, *Democracy in America*, 1:445.

2. Alexis de Tocqueville, *The Republic of the United States of America*, trans. Henry Reeve (New York: A. S. Barnes, 1956), 362.

3. Thurgood Marshall, *Thurgood Marshall: His Speeches, Writings, Arguments, Opinions, and Reminiscences*, ed. Mark V. Tushnet (Chicago: Lawrence Hill, 2001), 217.

4. James Baldwin, Canadian television interview, 1960. See www.youtube.com/watch?v=cplZdcp0fQY.

INDEX

Calvin Baker is the author of four novels, including *Dominion*, which was a finalist for the Hurston-Wright Award; *Grace*; *Naming the New World*; and *Once Two Heroes*. He has taught in Columbia University's Graduate School of the Arts; in the English Department at Yale University; and at the University of Leipzig, where he held the Picador Chair in American Studies. His nonfiction work has appeared in *BookPost*, *Harper's*, and the *New York Times Magazine*.